THE CIO
EDGE

OTHER BOOKS IN THE GARTNER, INC./
HARVARD BUSINESS REVIEW PRESS SERIES

The Real Business of IT
by Richard Hunter and George Westerman

*Mastering the Hype Cycle: How to Choose the Right Innovation
at the Right Time*
by Jackie Fenn and Mark Raskino

IT Risk: Turning Business Threats into Competitive Advantage
by George Westerman and Richard Hunter

*IT and the East: How China and India Are Altering the Future
of Technology and Innovation*
by James M. Popkin and Partha Iyengar

*Multisourcing: Moving Beyond Outsourcing to Achieve Growth
and Agility*
by Linda Cohen and Allie Young

The New CIO Leader: Setting the Agenda and Delivering Results
by Marianne Broadbent and Ellen S. Kitzis

*Heads Up: How to Anticipate Business Surprises and Seize
Opportunities First*
by Kenneth G. McGee

THE CIO EDGE

LEADERSHIP SKILLS
YOU NEED TO DRIVE RESULTS

GRAHAM WALLER

GEORGE HALLENBECK

KAREN RUBENSTRUNK

HARVARD BUSINESS REVIEW PRESS

Boston, Massachusetts

Library of Congress Cataloging-in-Publication Data

Waller, Graham.
    The CIO edge : seven leadership skills you need to drive results /
Graham Waller, George Hallenbeck, Karen Rubenstrunk.
        p. cm. — (Gartner)
    ISBN 978-1-4221-6637-6 (hardcover : alk. paper)   1. Leadership.
2. Chief information officers.   3. Executive ability.   I. Hallenbeck,
George.   II. Rubenstrunk, Karen.   III. Title.
    HD57.7.W352 2010
    658.4'092—dc22

                                                            2010011656

The paper used in this publication meets the requirements of the American
National Standard for Permanence of Paper for Publications and Docu-
ments in Libraries and Archives Z39.48-1992.

Graham:

To my amazing wife Patty

and to my parents, Sheila and John,

to whom I'm forever thankful.

George:

I would like to thank my wonderful

wife Kate for her understanding,

encouragement, and support.

Karen:

To my amazing husband Chuck,

for his unwavering love and his consistent

faith in me . . . and for never letting me

take myself too seriously.

CONTENTS

INTRODUCTION

SOFT SKILLS YIELD HARD RESULTS

L ET'S BEGIN WITH THE GOOD NEWS. There has never been a more energizing time to be a chief information officer, or CIO. Technology is the single most powerful enabling force available in business today—a tool executives and boards of directors increasingly recognize for its potential.

But be careful what you wish for! We now must meet those heightened expectations. Answering the question, "How can CIOs best deliver on the promise of IT?" is what this book is all about, and we begin by building on what you already know.

CIOs understand they need to manage IT processes in order to deliver results and to meet key expectations. They also understand the need to lead people in order to deliver on those goals. However, what many don't understand—and indeed what we didn't fully understand ourselves before we started our research—is the incredibly important interplay between the two.

Focusing on leadership and people skills—the "soft" things that many CIOs tend to minimize in their quest to keep up with their day-to-day responsibilities of managing IT—is in fact the biggest determinate of their success, or failure.

In the pages ahead, we will not only identify which specific skills are the most important but also explain: (1) how you can develop them and (2) why there is a huge payoff—both professionally *and personally*—if you do.

Soft skills yield hard results. We kept returning to this observation throughout our careers. Whether we were implementing IT-enabled projects, heading a CIO practice, coaching CIOs, or working with CEOs and boards on CIO hiring and talent development, this thought kept coming back to us. It seemed that those five words—soft skills yield hard results—always explained why a project succeeded. Conversely, the absence of those soft skills invariably was the reason it failed.

It didn't matter whether the company was introducing new hardware, implementing a major business initiative, or trying to turn around an IT organization; the harbinger of success was always the same. If the CIO had a good working relationship with everyone involved, from the business sponsors to vendors to colleagues organizationwide, the project invariably worked. Those soft people skills carried the day. If there was discord, strained relationships, or personal or professional opposition going in, you might as well have called off the whole thing before it began. There was never going to be a happy ending. Time after time, it was clear that soft skills yielded hard results.

When we observed success, it was not that the smartest people or the best technologists were promoted first. Instead, the IT executives who had the best relationships and could earn "followership"—not only with their employees, but more importantly with their business partners within and outside the organization—rose through the ranks the fastest. Most importantly, they were *perceived*—particularly by their business peers

---

All CIOs must deliver results. What distinguishes the best is how they do it: through people, by people, and with people.

throughout the enterprise—as successful leaders. That's no small thing, as you know.

In contrast, good CIOs often complete their projects on time and on budget. Networks are available when needed. Data is valid and secure. And yet, the *perceived* view of IT isn't great within the CIOs' companies. Executives outside the department point to business process changes that weren't supported or claim that all the discussions with IT are about cost when the focus should be business enablement. The net takeaway, despite a CIO's accomplishments, is that the IT department in general, and the CIO in particular, is frequently perceived as being out of sync with the rest of the organization. And all too often, perception is reality.

But we observed the CIOs with the best people skills did not suffer from this perception, because they used their soft skills to influence expectations well ahead of when priorities were set or a project began. Before a dime was budgeted, or staff time allocated, they were meeting with their colleagues, engaging in candid two-way conversations that defined what success would look like. Then they delivered against the expectations they helped set. As a result, the organization felt the investment of time and money in IT was worth it.

Soft skills produced hard results. This observation gave us an almost sixth sense that allowed us to predict whether a new project would succeed or flame out—and whether someone newly minted in the CIO role was destined for superstardom or soon would be looking for work. But for the longest time, we never really realized the full power of this insight as a way to help CIOs develop, improve, and ultimately excel in their role.

Then we got to talking during a break in a conference where we were presenting separately. After catching up, the conversation turned to questions that had been troubling us. If the successful application of IT is critical to an organization's success—and just about everyone believes it is—then why are so many CIOs still held in low esteem by CXOs (senior executives with *chief* in their title)? Why does the rest of the organization all too often remain skeptical about the performance of its IT department in general and the CIO specifically? In short, if there's been so much written about IT best practices, why are so few CIOs perceived by colleagues, boards, and CEOs as great leaders in their own right, continuously delivering great value to the business?

We didn't come up with an answer then and there. But we promised to spend a great deal of time working on an answer in order to help CIOs (and aspiring CIOs) better deliver on the immense promise of IT, something that is a passion of all three of us. Three years and countless hours of research, in-depth interviews, and collaboration later, the result is what you hold in your hands.

THE RESEARCH STARTED HERE

We began by asking the most basic question of all: How do we describe a superior chief information officer? Our answer was that great CIOs are inspirational leaders, consistently deliver results, exceed expectations of key stakeholders, and maximize the business value delivered via technology. Having agreed on the definition, we then asked the same question you would: What skills must a CIO have to do those four things?

When the question was asked that way, we thought of the CIOs who, we knew, fit the definition. What set them apart from the average executive? We noticed a clear pattern of people orientation, collaboration, and inclusiveness, but can excelling at soft skills mean excelling at being a high-performing CIO? We felt that the best CIOs employed soft skills to produce hard results. But could that really be the best explanation for their success? It felt right. But if we applied science to the problem, would we arrive at the same answer?

To find out, your authors joined forces. Karen and George brought the full resources of Korn/Ferry International (KFI), the world's premier provider of executive talent management solutions, to the problem. Graham harnessed the power of Gartner, Inc., the global leader in CIO and information technology research and advice. The melding of KFI's deep empirical data on leadership competencies (over one million executives studied) with Gartner's research on IT trends and the evolution of the CIO role would give us a unique and data-driven insight into the makeup of a high-performing CIO.

Once we had established a data-based profile for CIO success, we then set out to interview the best CIOs. Some of the high-performing CIOs were identified according to their results from KFI's leadership assessment tool; others we identified through recommendations from respected leaders throughout our global networks. We nominated still others on the basis of personal knowledge. Throughout, we cross-checked all of the above with the best available research from outside sources and through speaking with their peers and subordinates—we needed to make sure we were not drinking our own Kool-Aid. As we described in the appendix, we didn't prejudge anything. We simply asked all the CIOs about themselves, their leadership style, how they saw their priorities, how they got work done, and where they spent their time. There was nothing special about our questions, but there was surely something special in their answers. In the person's own way, each of these high performers told us that the key is people leadership.

As P&G's Filippo Passerini (president, global business services, and CIO) put it, "No amount of technology can replace the power of motivated and energized people. That's particularly true if your mission is to make a real difference as CIO, to create value via applying IT, to becoming a true strategic partner for the company versus having IT be relegated to a 'commodity' function. If that's your goal—and it is mine—people are central to transforming the way we do business. IT becomes more of a people business than a technology one. That's why my first focus is on people."[1]

Again, this makes sense. We all share increasingly similar core technology and best management practices. What varies most from CIO to CIO is how they lead, influence, inspire, and work with the people all around them. It follows, then, that this variable would be the biggest determinate of success. The simple diagrams in the figures help illuminate why that is the case.

THE PROBLEM: A LEADERSHIP VOID

In executing his or her day-to-day responsibilities, every CIO runs the IT organization via an increasingly common set of management systems (figure I-1). Even though it is not the most exciting aspect of the role, disciplined IT management practices are the very foundation for having the IT house in order and are consequently a prerequisite for any CIO's success in today's world. Couple that with the need to leverage IT to improve business processes and business performance, and you have a fairly good idea of the foundational aspects of the CIO role.[2]

FIGURE I-1

The management side of the CIO role

Beyond managing IT and applying business acumen, there is hardly a CIO who does not agree—at least intellectually—that providing leadership is a responsibility central to the CIO role. Leadership is about change and doing things differently; it requires setting a vision and inspiring others to follow. Core leadership characteristics are depicted in figure I-2.

As we said earlier in this chapter, however, there is a great interplay between management systems and leading people—the intersection where superior results are created, or not. Indeed, the dependence of CIO success on people leadership is often poorly understood and underappreciated.

Unfortunately, we all too often see CIOs giving extremely short shrift to the people-leadership part of the job. Whether it's due to the relentless management pressures of the position, unwitting undervaluing of the merits of "the people thing," or a lack of the requisite skills, the results are painfully clear. We observe the frustration of CIOs who feel neither heard nor

FIGURE I-2

The people side of the CIO leadership role

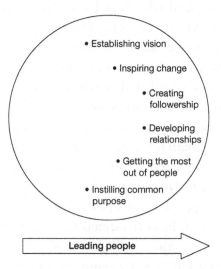

- Establishing vision
- Inspiring change
- Creating followership
- Developing relationships
- Getting the most out of people
- Instilling common purpose

Leading people

FIGURE I-3

Underdeveloped people leadership constrains results

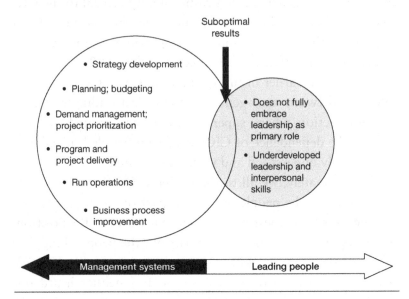

understood, who work tirelessly and sacrifice much personally but receive little thanks in return, and who struggle to meet the rising expectations of demanding business partners. As depicted in figure I-3, an underdeveloped leadership capability under-mines the capacity to optimize critical relationships and IT management processes alike and ultimately constrains or totally impedes CIOs' ability to deliver results.

Our research revealed that while a void in leadership is often a fatal flaw, it does not have to be the case. A CIO today must excel in two roles. *Only when you master the two halves of the job—the management system and associated business acumen on the one hand, and people leadership and the associ-ated interpersonal skills on the other—can you deliver high per-formance and superior results* (see figure I-4).

Indeed, it is the ability to astutely leverage interpersonal lead-ership at the intersection of these disciplines that distinguishes high-performing CIOs. For example, while all CIOs create a

FIGURE I-4

Maximizing people leadership maximizes results

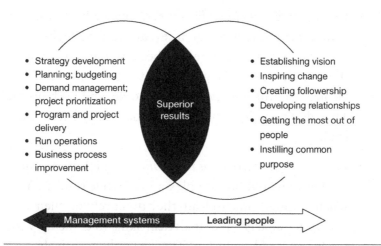

strategy, it is the high performers who have a vision that truly compels the desired actions. While all CIOs implement systems, it is the high performers who collaboratively partner to drive all the business process and cultural changes needed to maximize the business value of those systems. In short, leadership and interpersonal skills applied on the right act as a force enabling and amplifying the results of the processes and business knowledge on the left.

THE ANSWER: THE CIO EDGE

While saying the best CIOs excel at people leadership is a necessary starting point, that statement is insufficient to help you know what to do or how to do it. As our three years of data-driven research and field work came to a close, we distilled it down to the behavioral patterns and key skills we believe are the most critical to your success. The data (for an overview of the supporting research, see the appendix) and our interviews reveal that the best CIOs approach the role in a specific and predictable way. Specifically, high-performing CIOs distinguish themselves by mastering the following seven skills:

- *Committing to being a leader first.* Everything else comes second. Our research reveals that the highest-performing CIOs are effective because they embrace the idea that everything they need to accomplish will be achieved through people, by people, and with people. They don't pay lip service to that idea. They live it. They lead.

- *Leading differently than they think.* A high-performing CIO is an incredibly complex and creative thinker. Yet when it comes time to lead, they don't rely on their superior "smarts" and analytical skills to come up with the best possible solution. They act collaboratively.

- *Embracing their softer side.* Effective CIOs manage the paradox of gaining more influence by letting go of control and allowing themselves to be vulnerable. In turn, that vulnerability enables them to create deep, personal connections—connections that provide the ability to inspire people both inside and outside their organization.

- *Forging the right relationships to drive the right results.* This skill may not be surprising. But the following observation may be. Great CIOs spend a greater percentage of their time and energy managing relationships that exist sideways: with internal peers, external suppliers, and customers.

- *Practicing communication mastery.* All ways and always. The best CIOs know that their colleagues—especially the people who work for them—are always watching. These executives understand they are always on stage. They take advantage of that situation by constantly reiterating core messages and

FIGURE I-5

The **CIO edge**

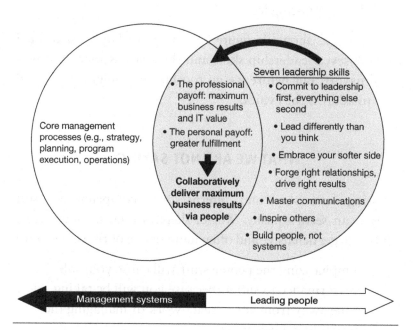

values. Through their focus on clarity, consistency, authenticity, and passion, they make sure their message is not only understood but also felt. They want to communicate a feeling that compels people to take the right actions.

- *Inspiring others.* In exchange for a regular paycheck, most people will give you an adequate performance. But they will only give you their best work if they believe they are involved in something greater than themselves. The best CIOs make it clear that their employees are involved in a greater good and that their contributions are meaningful and valued.

- *Building people, not systems.* By developing people all around them, these CIOs increase their capability and capacity to deliver results. They also know that leaving behind the next generation of leaders is the best thing they can do for the organization—it will be their lasting legacy.

Indeed, as shown in figure I-5, *The CIO Edge* is dedicated to these seven leadership skills and their professional and personal payoff. But before we go too far, now might be a good time to address the cynics.

WHAT WE ARE NOT SAYING

Stressing leadership and interpersonal competencies—soft skills—can seem squishy. Worse, skeptics (and less-than-great CIOs) can get defensive and often jump to one of two objections:

1. Emphasizing the people stuff will cause your job performance to suffer (because you will be taking time away from your "real" work of managing the technology investment).

2. Any decision to concentrate on soft skills will result in you being branded "soft" yourself.

In light of all the research we have done, we fervently believe that none of this is true. Indeed, a clear pattern from our interviews showed that the best CIOs, the ones who excel at people leadership, also set the most aggressive goals and hold their people accountable to the highest performance standards.

And even though the best CIOs are open and caring and relate well, they have no reluctance to fire people who underperform. These leaders recognize that not only is it best for the employee involved—if things aren't working out, it does not help either party to prolong the misery—but it is also unfair to the rest of the team to carry someone who can't contribute.

Even more pronounced is their zero tolerance for those who do not exhibit the key values and behaviors such as teamwork, integrity, and accountability—behaviors deemed central to the culture being fostered. Effective CIOs fully understand the toxic effect that just one bad apple can have when it comes to these core values. By allowing such behaviors to continue, they give tacit approval, hence undermining their very leadership credibility.

Intriguingly, because the best leaders excel at the people-related issues, they can move quickly when it is time to make a change. They have the absolute belief, conviction, and fortitude that they must make the hard people decisions for the organization to reach its full potential.

So the first misconception we need to clear up is that people with great soft skills are soft themselves. *The data shows the exact opposite.* Great CIOs take on the toughest challenges, are accountable, and do not tolerate a victim mentality (e.g., "no one knows how hard we work"; "we would be successful, if only *they* would let us").

Here's the second potential misunderstanding we want to address. We are not saying that people skills are all you need. First and foremost, you need to be able to *deliver* (i.e., stable operations and projects on time and on budget). You must understand your company's business model and the levers that drive growth and profitability within the competitive landscape. And, of course, you need to know what's on the technological horizon. But those are all the price of entry in the same way that an understanding of how to balance a budget and make financial trade-offs are things the CFO is assumed to know how to do.

Mastering the soft skills isn't a replacement for the core requirements of your job. It is instead a powerful enabler and an amplifying force that allows you to exceed expectations and maximize the value from IT.

The best CIOs embrace their soft side—without being soft themselves.

HOW THIS BOOK CAN HELP YOU

So why keep reading?

Your success, and in some cases your professional survival, will be strongly linked to your ability to shape and ultimately exceed the constantly morphing—and challenging—expectations of constituents internal and external to your company. Further, if IT is going to be a strategic partner and high-value contributor (versus the "commodity," low-value support function that Filippo Passerini alluded to earlier), then the CIO must be a great leader. And the pressure for you to fulfill that role is only going to increase. For example, while we have always had to get work done through others, as a result of the hyperconnected enterprise that we will detail in chapter 1, the "others" (both internally and externally) are increasingly not within our direct control. Not only may they be located halfway round the world, but they may also report to different departments or, increasingly, to other companies that are your strategic partners. In this kind of environment, you lead not by issuing orders, but by persuading and influencing, and you must know how to do that extremely well.

None of this has gone unnoticed by boards and the members of the C-suite responsible for hiring CIOs. They are *increasingly demanding their CIOs to be leaders first, and domain specialists second*.

There is one last benefit we want to address. Leading in a way that emphasizes soft skills will help alleviate the burnout and work-life balance issues that plague many IT professionals. Not only will it relieve some of the relentless demands you face—since you will be developing your people to the point where they can take over many of your day-to-day responsibilities—but the job will become more fulfilling since you know your legacy will be the evolution of the next generation of IT leadership.

So your work life will improve significantly—you will (finally) have the opportunity to deploy IT to the best possible advantage of your organization, if you make our seven skills your own. And your personal life will improve as well. We mention this last point for a particular reason. Many extremely talented IT people *don't* strive to become CIOs, because they believe the job has to be all-consuming. The best CIOs prove that this does not have to be the case.

WHAT'S AHEAD?

Here's how the book will lay out from here.

Remember figure I-5? We will begin at the beginning and explain why the approach in chapter 1, "Commit to Leadership First, Everything Else Second," must be your number-one priority. We explain why you cannot underestimate the importance of this step and how the people skills that will give you an edge today will be even more important in the years ahead.

In chapter 2, "Lead Differently Than You Think," we will unveil why, smart and as talented as you are, when it comes to taking action, you must lead collaboratively. That new way of thinking about your role and new way of leading will require you to pay more attention to your people-leadership skills. How you can learn to do that effectively makes up the central part of the book: chapter 3, "Embrace Your Softer Side"; chapter 4, "Forge Right Relationships, Drive Right Results"; chapter 5, "Master Communications: Always and All Ways"; chapter 6, "Inspire Others"; and chapter 7, "Build People, Not Systems." We spend a lot of time on these people skills for two reasons. First, for many people, these skills do not come naturally, and second, even among CIOs with good people skills, our research shows there is substantial room for improvement. While there are, of course, other books that address people and leadership skills, we believe ours is unique in its depth of data-based research focused solely on uncovering and sharing the unique skills of the high-performing CIO.

We conclude by discussing the payoff from all this, not only professionally (chapter 8, "The Professional Payoff: Delivering

Business Results") but personally as well (chapter 9, "The Personal Payoff"). We show you what you can do starting today to move into the ranks of tomorrow's best CIOs.

We like the flow, but you don't have to be bound by it. Skip ahead. Or read the chapters in any order you like. (We deliberately made them modular.) You picked up this book because you thought it could make you better at your job. We are convinced it can.

What makes a great CIO is no longer a secret. Apply the insights we have discovered—the CIO edge—to deliver significant value to your organization and to create a lasting legacy.

Let's begin.

COMMIT TO LEADERSHIP FIRST, EVERYTHING ELSE SECOND

DELIVERING RESULTS THROUGH PEOPLE, BY PEOPLE, AND WITH PEOPLE

When Tom Tabor, CIO of Highmark, a large U.S.-based health insurer, was chosen to head the technology department, many within IT were surprised. He wasn't the most senior person, and while his technical skills were excellent, there were certainly as many people in the department who knew as much as—if not more than—he did about IT. So why did he get the job?

"When Tom was chosen, he wasn't chosen for the future of technology; he was chosen for the future of technology's impact within Highmark," says company CEO Ken Melani. "And Tom was always one of those executives who got things done. Regardless of the situation, he managed to get people to work together and be focused. We needed his talent in managing through people; otherwise, we would have never fully optimized the millions we spent on technology."[1]

Melani's comment sums up beautifully why your company is looking for you to be a leader. Although you have always heard that "the CIO is uniquely situated to view the entire enterprise," today's organization increasingly wants and needs you to add value to what you see.

It is not that your management and technical skills aren't valued. It's that they are now viewed as necessary but insufficient. The company needs you to do more. It needs you to be a leader.

For while technology has huge potential to transform business performance, its power can only be unlocked via people. And getting a diverse group of people, both across the enterprise and outside its four walls, to deliver on the best IT-enabled opportunities requires leadership.

As Melani said, that is something CEOs and boards of directors increasingly look for in their CIOs. Dean Harrison, CEO of Northwestern Memorial Hospital, underscores the point: "We expect our senior leaders to be institutional leaders who can transcend their roles and skills beyond their traditional areas of expertise. As an example, we recently promoted Tim Zoph, our CIO, to a senior vice president and expanded his portfolio from developing and implementing our technology strategy to helping advance our entire organization with additional responsibilities."[2]

The best CIOs do everything in their power to fulfill those expectations. They make leadership their number-one job.

IF WE ALL have access to the same technology, the same management practices, and the same labor pool, why is it that some CIOs are phenomenally successful while others merely muddle along (or worse, get overwhelmed)? After personally interviewing hundreds of CIOs and analyzing the vast research base on which this book is based (see appendix), we found that the answer was quite clear: the highest-performing CIOs are effective because they embrace the idea that everything they need to accomplish will be achieved through people, by people, and with people.

Great CIOs thus spend an inordinate amount of time providing people within the organization the following: vision, common purpose, inspiration, clear expectations, development, and an environment where the people can successfully deliver results. In other words, the CIOs lead. Understanding that everything they do flows from this, they put leadership at the forefront of all their efforts. And you must, too.

This is an important point. Virtually every CIO we talked to agreed *intellectually* that the idea of people leadership—that they need to create an environment that allows people to do their best work—is critically important to their own success. But as we discussed in the introduction, intellectual understanding is not the same as committing to action.

Despite their best efforts, CIOs who don't fully commit to people leadership in both thought and action don't get the results they hope for. It is easy to spot these CIOs. They talk about the importance of people leadership, but only dedicate a very small percentage of their time to pure people issues such as relationship development across the company, shaping shared expectations, or mentoring and coaching direct reports. Or these executives are inconsistent in their leadership style, collaborating when it's easy, but acting authoritatively under pressure or when peers or subordinates don't share their view.

They say they want to influence and persuade, not order, but they push back against the idea of spending the time and energy it takes to build the deep, interpersonal relationships that encourages strong, lasting influence. They get compliance,

---

A POTENTIALLY UNSETTLING QUESTION

Are you so consumed in executing the core IT management tasks that you are unable to fulfill your primary role as a leader—the biggest role your people, peers, and enterprise need you to play?

---

not commitment. Not surprisingly, then, these CIOs may deliver the project, achieve the objective, or solve the problem, but they are rarely perceived as being able to do more (such as shape the company's vision or be true organizational leaders).

Let's try to underscore this distinction between giving lip service to people leadership and actually doing it. Table 1-1 shows the change in the hardworking CIO who has committed to putting people leadership first. If you identify more often with the column on the left, you may have admitted a need to change, but have yet to commit.

TABLE 1-1

Commitment to leadership first: What it looks like

My mind-set	Before	After
How I define my role	Manage IT function efficiently and effectively to deliver reliable IT projects and services.	Lead people collaboratively across functions, inspiring others to achieve extraordinary business results via technology.
How I define success relative to the IT organization	Recognized for leading a well-run IT organization, receiving solid customer satisfaction ratings.	Recognized as a business leader whose organization is perceived as a valued partner in achieving results.
How I manage expectations	React to changing expectations.	Help shape shared expectations.
My relationship with the C-suite	Maintain mostly formal transactional relationships, primarily through involvement at periodic meetings such as monthly status, program update, or annual planning.	Build trusted, fully collaborative relationships with the majority of C-suite members, including unplanned, informal meetings to discuss opportunities and issues as they arise.
My relationship with the board	Uphold IT-related fiduciary responsibility and reporting requirements.	Go beyond IT-related fiduciary responsibility to become a trusted adviser and personal confidant on key business opportunities and risk issues.
How I define my team and think about my role within the team	Manage the efforts of the core IT team to meet and deliver on business expectations.	Integrate multiple key relationships (both inside and outside IT—up, down, and sideways) into a cohesive, extended team to achieve superior business results.

My mind-set	Before	After
How I think about and execute the people side of my role	Effectively manage core people processes such as recruiting, training, and performance reviews.	Lead, inspire, and develop people so that they can unleash their full potential and drive business results.
How I allocate my time	Strive to allocate needed time to leadership, people, and strategic matters, but often consumed by tactical matters and the need to react to immediate problems.	Focus efforts on developing IT direct reports (and the broader IT organization) so that the department can operate independently, allowing more time to concentrate on leadership and strategy.
How I view my legacy	To have led a well-run IT organization capable of consistently delivering complex projects and managing IT operations.	To have developed people and created a self-sustaining organization that continues to deliver value and exceed expectations well beyond my tenure with the organization.

If the table didn't help in underscoring the difference between saying you believe in being a leader and actually doing it, consider taking a rearview-mirror look. When you left your last position (or when you leave this one), did (or will) your superiors immediately think of the struggle they would have deciding between the multiple direct reports of yours that were all highly qualified to succeed you, or did (or will) they come up empty-handed? A CIO who has fully committed to putting people leadership first rarely leaves an IT organization that does not have viable and valuable successors within it.

THE "AHA" MOMENT

Some CIOs need an "aha" moment to understand the importance of being a leader. The light bulb goes on over their heads

The best CIOs fundamentally believe that the only way to be successful is to excel at "the people thing."

one day, and they say, "I get it." That's what happened to Randy Spratt, executive vice president, chief technology officer, and chief information officer of McKesson, a health-care company with $90 billion in revenues.

> While we were working a multiyear program to drive consistent, world-class support to the rest of the organization, I came across this piece of research that said, in essence, financial performance comes from customer loyalty because if customers don't come back to you and don't talk positively about you to others, sooner or later, your business will decline. Where does customer loyalty come from? From repeated, not single, but repeated satisfaction with the products, services, and interactions with the company. And what is the only way that can come about? Through your people. They're either deeply jazzed about building great products that meet customer needs and taking care of the customer, or they're not.
>
> There is only one thing that creates an environment which will get them jazzed. Leadership. How you create your incentive programs; how you recognize and reward them; how you develop them. The pace, the tone, everything you do winds up at your financial results through the pathway of how your people behave.
>
> That "aha" moment completely changed the way I looked at leading, because I realized it starts with the people. Financial results are trailing indicators.[3]

What Spratt identified is what many fail to recognize—effective leadership begins with people first, and through them, results follow.

Others among the best CIOs we interviewed concluded that people leadership needed to come first only after they witnessed the results from doing it. Through trial and error, they eventually learned that leadership was their number-one priority and realized that once they invested the majority of their time there, their department's performance improved dramatically.

There's an obvious reason why many CIOs have trouble embracing the concept that being a leader is more important than managing IT. It's simply counterintuitive to just about anything they have been rewarded for earlier in their career.

The path you take to this realization doesn't particularly matter. What does matter is understanding that your number-one job isn't mastering the technology. It is providing collaborative, participative leadership through which you create the relationships, commitments, shared visions, and common purpose that enable success.

Given the unique role the CIO plays, that isn't surprising. Think about your job for a minute. First, you are a service provider to just about every other part of the business. You have to simultaneously manage the relationships with each business unit, each of which has its own needs, style, and capabilities, while you look out for the greater good of the enterprise. As one CIO said, "I have to find a way to work with them much more than they have to find a way to work with me. If I ran a business unit and it was producing significant profits, I might be able to get away with being a jerk. Since I am not, I need to find ways to work productively with every single department in the organization—meeting their needs and ours."

Second, change within IT is often more complex and intertwined across the enterprise than it is for most other functions. Without exemplary people skills, building an understanding and support of the difference can have dire consequences for the organization—and your career.

One CIO gave us an excellent example. "If an ad campaign fails and the board takes our marketing department to task, they might fire the VP of marketing, maybe fire the ad agency and hire a different one, but after six months and an investment of fresh money, we are on to a whole new marketing strategy," he said. "But if you need to change an aging ERP [enterprise resource

---

Think about how others—your boss, business unit leaders, direct reports—would weigh in on your people-leadership skills. Would they describe you as an inspirational business leader, one to whom they naturally turn regarding their most pressing challenges? If not, what impact do their perceptions have on your ability to exceed expectations and deliver value?

---

planning system] or correct a poorly implemented CRM [customer relationship management] system, the IT and business changes will take years and cost millions of dollars. If I can't call on people skills to get that difference understood, I'm toast."

NO EXCUSES

As we went about doing research for this book, one theme constantly reoccurred: high-performing CIOs repeatedly told us you can't tolerate excuses for failing to deliver on expectations and delivering value. You can't complain about the pressures you are under or how your business partners do not understand IT or have a different view of the priorities. The best CIOs said that if you want to earn the same level of respect accorded other parts of the organization, you need to make sure you hold yourself, and your department, to the same standards that they are judged against.

Too often we have not done that, and as a result, the way IT is viewed has suffered, a point that Barbra Cooper, group vice president and CIO for Toyota Motor Sales U.S.A., hammered home for us. "You know why the perception of IT has suffered for thirty years?" she asks rhetorically. "It's almost as if we've swallowed a victim-mentality pill. You know, 'Poor me. People don't understand how hard my job is.' That kind of thinking is simply not acceptable if you want to be taken seriously by the organization."[4]

P&G's Filippo Passerini is equally blunt:

One thing that must be forbidden in our world is self-commiseration, the idea that people don't understand how good a job we are doing, or that they don't appreciate us. That is absolutely nonsense. It would be as if P&G said the reason our sales are off is because customers don't understand how much care we put into them. That wouldn't be our customers' fault. It would be ours, because in the end, it doesn't matter how hard we try. It is how much we sell. In IT, the mind-set has got to be the same. It is up to us to shape our destiny; it is completely up to us.

Passerini, who was trained as an engineer, is arguing that CIOs must think like a business leader and not just a technologist, and he concedes that is not necessarily easy for someone who has come up through the IT ranks:

People with a technical background, like myself, tend to think in binary terms. Either-or. You can either have lower cost or better quality; speed or power. But if you are running a business unit, as I did, you are expected every year to deliver bigger sales volumes, increase your market share, *and* increase your profit. If you think about it, those three—profit, volume, and share—are in conflict. Because if you want to increase profit, you will increase price—but if you increase price, chances are, volume will drop. So in business, it is not either-or. It is "and, and, and."

We need to shift the thinking in IT. We have to stop saying we can reduce cost or increase speed. We need to stop telling our colleagues that if we increase speed, the quality will be affected. We need to make our thinking "and, and, and"—that we can reduce cost, increase speed, and improve quality. At P&G, we have been doing this. We have been training IT people to have this business mind-set. We have managers who act pretty much like

---

The best CIOs expand their already well-honed technological mind-
set to think and act the same way as other good business leaders
within their organizations.

---

a brand manager with the rest of the company. They
are responsible for the creation of the service, running
the service, innovating the service, providing the service,
commercializing the service. So the skills that are required
are the ones of businesspeople.

Sony's CIO Shinji Hasejima sums up the no-excuses argument beautifully: "Instead of being reactive, CIOs must be
proactive. In the past, when IT was given too many tasks, it took
the easy way out by prioritizing. We on the IT side need to struggle more just like our business partners within the company—
doing much more with much less—or we cannot be true partners in the business."[5]

Up until now, we have focused on the internal factors that
are demanding that you become a leader first. But there are also
external factors that amplify this need.

WHY THE DEMAND FOR ADVANCED
LEADERSHIP WILL EXPLODE

If you are feeling that the pace of change is relentless, and you
are a person at the epicenter of making sure that your organization not only keeps up with it but also responds effectively:

1. You are right.

2. You are not alone.

For whether we view change through a social or business
lens, the underlying enabler, without doubt, has technology at

its core. Indeed, the speed with which information technology is reshaping the global economy and creating new forms of competition is staggering. It is not only enabling new business models but also challenging traditional management assumptions. And we are only just beginning.

By the nature of the CIO role, you sit, whether you like it or not, at the very eye of this storm, at the nexus of decisions and leadership actions. These decisions span an immense spectrum, from what personal productivity devices your organization will use, to what systems and people to deploy to ensure your organization can do business effectively around the world.

The complexity of these trends is increasing—in some cases exponentially—and we have a shortage of qualified business technology leaders to deal with them. As a result, the demand for advanced leadership will explode. A look at just a couple key factors you will have to face in the years ahead will explain why.

The Hyperconnected Enterprise

As the information economy takes permanent hold, the twenty-first-century organization is emerging, one that exists within a complex ecosystem filled with numerous intersections and interdependencies across suppliers, buyers, and customers worldwide. Gartner analyst Diane Morello calls it the *hyperconnected enterprise,* and it is easy to see why.

Let's start with the obvious. There are more outsourcing relationships, partnerships, and joint ventures than ever before. Whether focused on stimulating demand or providing increased channels to market your company's products, the increased connectivity and interdependence is rampant. And all this does not even take into account the growing influence of consumer and advocacy groups and the rise of social networking. When you add all this up, it is not hyperbole to say we have never before seen the likes of this kind of interconnectivity among stakeholders.

As this trend rolls across enterprises of all types, your job, as figure 1-1 depicts, will increasingly be part of an ecosystem that is beyond your direct control.

How do you function in this new environment? You start, as Kimberly-Clark's CIO Ramón Baez makes clear, by forging closer relationships with key partners both inside *and outside* your organization:

> Since we outsource and deal with multiple stakeholders, it is important that I get our partners just as excited about Kimberly-Clark as I do the people within our company. And I need to be just as collaborative with them. If I am not, it's going be very hard to influence some of the direction that we need to go.
>
> Dealing with people outside the corporation is going to become even more important in coming years. So what I am now dealing with—and expect to be dealing with to

FIGURE 1-1

The hyperconnected enterprise

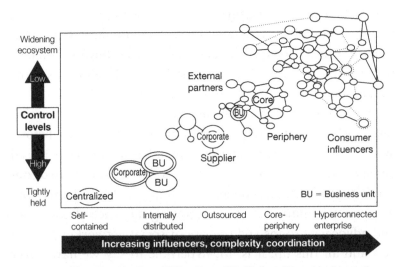

Source: Adapted from Diane Morello and Colleen Young, "The Big Bang: Demand for Advanced Leadership Explodes in the Connected World," Gartner conference presentation, October 2008.

> an even greater degree going forward—is managing
> diverse relationships both inside and outside our com-
> pany. That's a huge challenge for a lot of people. So
> what I'm trying to demonstrate to my IT folks is that,
> while it is true that they need to have technology experi-
> ence, they really need to master that skill of managing
> diverse relationships.[6]

That is a huge point. While you have always had to get
work done via others, the "others" have expanded radically
and are increasingly independent and outside your direct control. Given the increasing complexity of how business will get
done in the future, traditional command and control will be
dead. You will have to achieve results through your ability to
influence people. (This obviously will require a new set of
skills. We'll expand on this skill set in chapters 3 through 7.)

One more point before we move on. It's important that we
don't make the mistake of thinking that this highly complex,
hyperconnected enterprise exists only for the *Fortune* 100 global
companies. It's a trend we've seen across just about every enterprise and business. We mentioned Dean Harrison at the beginning of this chapter. You wouldn't think that a hospital system
geographically bounded by Chicago would be all that complex.
But the reality is that his company is reflective of most, regardless of size. Harrison describes the web of business relationships
at Northwestern Memorial:

> We've got sixteen hundred faculty members, seven hun-
> dred and fifty medical residents, and approximately seven
> thousand employees. Children's Memorial Hospital and
> the Rehabilitation Institute of Chicago are part of our
> medical center, as we all share a clinical affiliation with
> Northwestern University Feinberg School of Medicine.
> In addition, other critical relationships extend beyond our
> campus partners to include numerous vendors and suppli-
> ers that help us provide the safest care to our patients and

recruit and retain a workforce of talented and committed
people who share our values and that help us achieve
our vision. The management and delivery of health care
is a complex environment and benefits from strong
relationships.

The need for the advanced people-leadership skills described
throughout this book will become acute. The more complex
environment will expose leadership shortfalls like never before.
Organizations will be looking not only for people comfortable
with the increased complexity that they will face, but also
for those who can actually thrive in this kind of environment.
They need executives who can set direction, rather than those
who direct. Who can inspire and motivate a diverse team
beyond their immediate control. Who can lead in a participative way that fosters true buy-in and loyalty to common goals.
Who can establish a shared vision and then execute across
boundaries.

As Toyota's Cooper explains, "we are entering a future of
very fast-paced global change. In the past, IT was a service
provider and judged by how well it could come up with a solution that provided what the business wanted at a reasonable
price. But, as the line between business and IT begins to blur,
the question will be how well can IT represent the enterprise
across the entire supply chain, to use just one example, not just
how well it performs in its individual silo."

Globalization

We are only just beginning to grasp the extreme complexity of a
truly globalized marketplace. Increased connectivity, made possible by IT and the Internet, is removing many of the barriers
that previously constrained worldwide trade, communications,
employment, and social discourse. While the past decade's
multibillion-dollar investment in fiber-optic highways and
satellites has made the world flatter and smaller, management

practices are struggling to keep pace. Traditional approaches are too highly structured to cope with the rapidly changing environment of a global economy.

New success factors will require a more participative leadership style to navigate in a flat world. Prospering will demand a culturally sensitive environment that focuses on teamwork among internal operations and external constituencies.

Ford CIO Nick Smither provides us a great window into these trends, as he explains how they are playing out during the implementation of the ONE Ford business strategy that calls for a more globally integrated and leveraged business model. As Smither told us, for the IT organization to contribute to this strategy, "we must be able to optimize resources worldwide; whether they be our data centers, our people and distributed teams, or IT-enabled business processes such as global product development. This puts a premium on people who can lead and drive results at a global level, people who can work together with others transcending time zones and cultures to get the best out of diverse distributed teams. Obviously, these are skills that are in short supply."[7]

In response to this business need, Smither is leveraging Ford's long-standing talent development programs (designed to build both functional IT excellence and business acumen), adding an emphasis on global competencies. For example, people are being given longer-term (two- to three-year) developmental assignments; midterm "backpacking" assignments (typically six months where, for example, an India-based associate would be sent to the United States to gain experience there); and short-term "shadowing" (typically one week, where a European-based associate would travel with an Asia executive to gain insight into that part of the business and culture).

"Developing our people and making sure that they have the key competencies called for by our business strategy—such as being able to deliver globally—is absolutely key to our sustained success and ability to add value," says Smither.

As organizations become increasingly global—through expansion, joint ventures, and outsourcing—the CIO will need to develop leadership skills that transcend organizational, cultural, time, and distance boundaries. Learning not only how to survive but also how to capitalize on this global diversity will be a key to effective twenty-first-century leadership.

Michael Kollig, regional CIO at the Paris-based Danone Group, which is "committed to supplying healthy foods worldwide," agrees: "Working across cultures, it is my task, and that of my organization, to be relevant to others, regardless of where they are or what organization they are in. I push myself and am requiring of my people to maintain an emphasis on communications, openness, cultural sensitivity, and appreciation for unique needs."[8]

The implications for the CIO are clear. Combining and leveraging capabilities from global operations and disparate cultures will require a heightened set of leadership skills that are rich in cultural sensitivity and have the ability to build shared purpose, vision, and values across multiple time zones and cultures.

Evolving Consumer Expectations

The expectations your internal customers (i.e., your colleagues) have about what technology should be able to do is changing. This is especially true among Gen Xers and Gen Ys, those in their forties to early twenties.

They have profoundly different demands regarding technology, communication, technology-enabled collaboration, information access, and consumption . . . the list goes on. This conclusion was brought home to us when we asked a member of Generation Y, who seems to have a smart-phone implanted in her left hand, whether she saw the value of e-mail. She paused and eventually responded yes, "to send thank you messages to my friends' parents."

These colleagues, often called digital natives, who have now embraced the ease of use and information-rich experiences from Amazon.com, Google, eBay, Facebook, Twitter, and the like, are used to almost instant communication, thanks to things like text messaging, and are increasingly demanding these types of experiences in their professional lives. If they can find virtually whatever they need with a few clicks of a mouse during their off-hours, how come it takes so long to access the data that they need at work?

From your perspective as a CIO leader, this new generation creates both rich opportunities and significant challenges across an extremely broad spectrum. You need to not only

FIGURE 1-2

Committing to people leadership unlocks the full value potential of the organization to deliver results

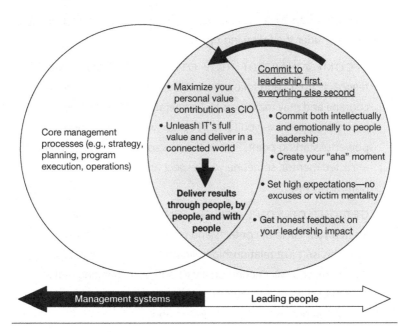

provide the type of personal productivity and collaborative environments they grew up in, but much more importantly, adapt your leadership style to get them to do their best work. They don't respond well to hierarchical approaches, hoarding of information, and being confined to silos. And they believe—correctly—that it is silly for you to expect them to ignore what they know about the next generation of consumers (since they are a member of that group), just because they work in IT and not marketing.

Regardless of how many of these trends are affecting your enterprise, as CIO, you must be capable of influencing others and moving them toward the right action, independent of their geography, placement on an organization chart, or view of technology. And committing to people leadership is the key step in doing just that, as you can see in figure 1-2.

CALL TO ACTION

If you have a ways to go until leadership is first and everything else is second, consider the following tips for development:

BECOME AWARE OF HOW OTHERS SEE YOU. Seek feedback, listen, and take action. Although these steps can take courage and may make you feel vulnerable, self-awareness of how others perceive you (or don't perceive you) as a leader is a powerful starting point. Part of the process can often be finding a trusted mentor, someone you respect and who can be brutally honest with you.

GET OUT OF YOUR OFFICE. Better yet, get out of IT. Stretch your circle of contacts and relations as far out as you can. This isn't just relationship building for its own sake. More and more, you will depend on a vast and ever-changing network of relationships to accomplish goals and make your vision a reality. The process takes time. Invest now.

REBALANCE YOUR FOCUS AND TIME ALLOCATION.
If you are consumed with IT management tasks and reacting
to issues, summon the courage to break the cycle. Commit to
carving out the time you need in order to lead—the primary role
those around you need you to play. Block out dedicated time on
your calendar to sharpen and apply the seven leadership skills
described in this book.

TRY A NEW LENS. As an experienced professional, you
have probably learned to look at challenges and opportunities
through the dual lenses of technology and business, but what
about people? As you encounter new situations, step back to
look at them from the perspective of "What are the implications
here from a people-leadership perspective?" Compare this point
of view to what you see from other perspectives, and see if new
insights start to emerge.

SUMMING UP

The key differentiator between the highest-performing CIOs and
ordinary ones is high performers' commitment to leadership
(manifested by their ability to exceed expectations and drive
value).

Getting people leadership right will not only produce oper-
ational excellence, but also unlock the full value potential of IT
and ultimately lead to your success as a CIO. Indeed, in view of
the macro trends discussed earlier in this chapter (and their
associated complexity and interdependencies), it is the only
way to do your job well.

Put another way, the only way to do your job successfully is
through people. If you aren't someone who both guides and
inspires others to get the right work done, you will ultimately fail.

You have to truly commit at a deep, emotional level to leading through people, versus just intellectually grasping this
point. There is just too much for you to do alone.

The primary responsibility of the CIO is *not* to be the foremost expert on technology. It is to exceed business expectations and maximize IT's value contribution. The highest performers understand the only way to achieve both is via people, a relentless and passionate focus on people.

It isn't easy to make the commitment to leadership first, but every high-performing CIO said it was more than worth the effort.

LEAD DIFFERENTLY
THAN YOU THINK

THINK ANALYTICALLY, ACT COLLABORATIVELY

It is a very simple example, but it makes an extremely important point. Listen as Stephen Fugale explains how he made the mental shift from knowing exactly what needed to be done and plowing ahead, to determining a course of action that would guarantee that the right solution would not only be implemented, but also embraced.

I had changed industries, moving from insurance and employee benefits at CIGNA Group Insurance, to becoming the CIO at Villanova University.

Once I got there, it was apparent to everyone that our phone system needed to be replaced. I had what I thought was an excellent solution in mind. Coming from the industry I came from, and the role I played there, I believe I had enough personal credibility and technology know-how that if I picked a phone system and then recommend it to the people who had to approve it, it probably would have been authorized. But instead of acting on my own, I created a steering committee made up of influential people from every part of the university who were heavy phone users. These were people who had credibility across the campus. We in the IT department did our due diligence, and periodically, I would update and present our findings to them.

What I was doing was engaging with people who were trusted throughout the university, people who I thought would help communicate to everyone we were making the right decision.

I had them review requirements. I let them know who we were eliminating and why. They didn't do any of the actual due diligence, visiting vendors or whatever. But I engaged them.

If I hadn't done all that, would we have ended up recommending the same system? Probably. But the decision may not have been accepted. People who were not consulted might have objected because they felt slighted. Others could have voiced complaints simply because we were doing something new. And certainly, someone influential would have tried to delay the decision because they were convinced that they had a better idea.

But because we acted the way we did, none of that happened. Once we came to decision and implementation, it was one of the smoothest transitions this traditionally change-adverse community had undergone.[1]

HERE IS NEWS that won't stop the presses: the world is getting more complicated, digitized, and hyperconnected, and so the demand for CIOs who are technologically savvy has never been greater. Not that the high-performing CIO has to know the most about every technology, but he or she needs to have the grounding and experience in some important aspects of IT management. A CIO, along with his or her team, needs to define what is technically feasible and in what time frame; determine what it takes to implement the task at hand; manage the risks along the way; minimize cost and maximize performance; and, most importantly, demonstrate the smarts to combine technological know-how with business acumen to understand what is truly important.

And yet simply being smart and technologically savvy is not enough. While the top-performing CIOs can indeed think through and develop the absolute best mousetrap, they learn early on that they cannot lead by simply knowing the best answer. People are rarely moved by someone else's elegant solution. They are inspired when they feel included and connected to a vision they can relate to, when they believe they are contributing to something worthwhile, something that is bigger than them.

What all this means is that the superior intelligence that got you here (to a senior leadership position within the IT department) won't get you there—to a job where you can influence the entire enterprise to best leverage technology for business advantage. To achieve that goal, you will need to lead in a different style from how you think, as Fugale's experience shows. The best CIOs have figured out how to do just that. And equally important, they have learned—often the hard way—that smarts alone are not enough. You need more than intelligence to solve problems such as the trade-offs involved in maximizing a business unit and enterprise performance, or limited resources, or conflicting demands of various stakeholders. So it is not surprising that our research shows that a high-performing CIO is an incredibly smart, technologically savvy professional who also has the critically important, highly developed interpersonal skills required to do the job effectively.

The melding of extremely effective reasoning with stellar interpersonal skills sounds virtually impossible. And it would be, except for one fascinating thing: the best CIOs lead in ways that are very different from how they reason. While they use their superior analytical abilities to help derive the best possible

TECHNOLOGICAL SAVVY STILL MATTERS

Given our focus on people leadership throughout this book, a valid question is whether superior CIOs still need a solid technology foundation. The short answer is yes. Our interviews with top performers revealed that one element that complements their decision making is their grounding in technology.

Among the highest-performing CIOs we interviewed, over 90 percent had significant IT-related roles earlier in their careers, which gave them the foundation to understand how all the pieces fit together. Today, not one of them could code well if they had to, but they understand and have experience in making the networks, applications, business processes, vendors, and people work together. They have the technological savvy to distill hype from reality, to command the respect of the IT team, and to understand how to leverage technology for business advantage. This foundation provides context for their instinctual ability to synthesize the vast complexity and numerous options into optimum business-oriented solutions.

The key takeaway is this: with the dramatic increases in both the pace of change and the complexity of the operating environment for the CIO, a solid grounding in technology is absolutely essential.

---

solution, they act in a collaborative style. They seek out people to gain additional ideas that can help reinforce, refine, and improve the conclusions that emerged from their own analysis. Of course, as a result of this inclusiveness, they are also guiding and influencing others to come along with them.

This is very much a learned behavior among the highest-performing CIOs. Indeed, they often have to actively suppress their initial inclination to lead with the best mousetrap (i.e., an intellectually eloquent solution). Instead, they take the extra time and effort to include others, often shaping and fine-tuning the conclusion along the way. Not everyone took to this course of action naturally—or even liked doing it initially—but excellent CIOs came to understand they had to do it.

As Stein Tumert, CIO of Burger King Europe, Middle East and Africa, told us, "if you are going to create something new that will be embraced by others, you must be able to relate to people and build relationships that enable them to truly open up and share their best ideas, ideas which have the potential to substantially improve your own." This was not always Tumert's approach. Earlier in his career, he discovered the hard way that not everyone was willing to follow him, "even if I have the very best idea or storytelling skills." In working with a coach, Tumert realized he needed to dramatically change the way he listened. "In the past, when someone talked, I immediately began formulating a response, rather than listening. A coach helped me understand that listening was not just waiting to speak. Learning to listen was one way I learned to more effectively get the best input from everyone."[2]

Tumert's experience is typical of many CIOs who in the earlier stages of their careers were respected and rewarded for their intelligence and technical smarts. But as they matured and began scaling the ranks, they realized that being smart was not enough to get things done. And so they evolved from leading by intellect to leading through building and employing people skills. They came to see that while it is critically important to be intellectually smart, it is not the most effective strategy for getting people to follow them.

It's a fascinating—and vitally important—transformation. Let's spend some time explaining how and why it can come about so you can benefit as well.

HIGH PERFORMERS: CREATIVE
AND COMPLEX THINKERS

If we are going to say that the best CIOs lead differently from how they reason, it is helpful to truly understand both how they lead and how they think. Korn/Ferry International (KFI)

A POTENTIALLY UNSETTLING QUESTION

We all have times when we believe we absolutely understand the situation and know just how something should be done (a particular approach to governance, a prioritization of capital spending, a chosen software solution), and yet we can't get others to pledge their full support. If this describes you far too often, ask yourself this: is my leadership style focused on creating the perfect solution (i.e., the best mousetrap) or facilitating a solution that will be truly embraced and executed to drive results?

has dedicated significant resources to exploring what differentiates the thinking and leading styles of high performers. The company has assessed more than 1.4 *million* executives and developed an empirically sound benchmark for identifying a high performer. (KFI defines a high performer as one who statistically outperforms peers in career progression and salary within high-quality companies and who has established a track record of exceeding expectations through having his or her people deliver high-value solutions to the organization.)

High performers demonstrate distinctive patterns of thinking and leading. We'll start with their thinking style.

Thinking style is defined as how individuals drive to a decision when they are alone, unobserved, or with a very close group of colleagues. The research shows that thinking styles differ along two fundamental dimensions (figure 2-1):

1. How people use the data presented to them: just enough (low to moderate) or as much as possible (high)

2. How they go about creating options to pursue: focusing on a single solution (unifocused) or many possible solutions (multifocused)

FIGURE 2-1

Information use versus focus in styles

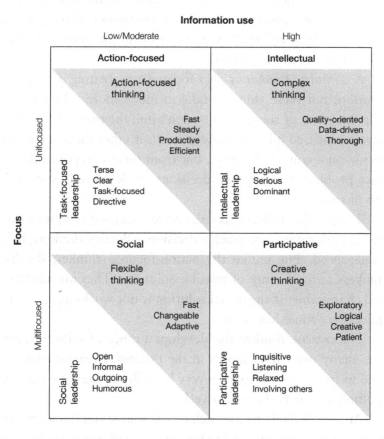

Source: Korn/Ferry International.

At the intersection of each category of information use and focus in figure 2-1, a different thinking style emerges. For example, complex thinkers seek out and use high amounts of information and are unifocused in their search for solutions. You will also notice that different leadership styles are also represented in the figure; we will deal with those a little later in the chapter. For now, let's dig a little deeper into each of the thinking styles.

An *action-focused thinker* uses just enough information to make a decision. This person moves toward a decision quickly, makes it, and moves on to the next task. People who employ this style value speed, efficiency, and consistency. Having made a decision, they will stick with it until overwhelming evidence shows it needs to be changed.

A *complex thinker* is also focused on creating a singular solution, but these thinkers take in much more information, from a variety of sources. They don't pull the trigger until they have considered all inputs. As a result, it takes them longer to decide on a course of action, but from their viewpoint, this is not a problem, because their decisions are designed to stand the test of time.

The *flexible thinker,* like the action-focused one, uses just enough information to reach a decision—flexible thinkers, too, value speed. But unlike the action-focused thinker, flexible thinkers create a range of possible solutions. They are adaptive and changeable. If the initial solution is not working, they will quickly try something else.

The *creative thinker* also develops a range of solutions, but uses many more data inputs in the process. Creative thinkers tend to frame every situation very broadly, taking into account multiple elements that may overlap.

Anyone is likely to use each of the four styles from time to time, but most people tend to favor the use of one or two of the styles across most situations. Our research shows the best CIOs primarily use the creative and complex thinking styles. Figure 2-2 reveals the relative weight (1 means a small degree of emphasis; 7 a great deal) that high-performing CIOs place on each of the four styles and what the approach tends to look like in action.

When faced with a decision, CIOs with this thinking pattern balance openness to new information with thoroughness and patience in vetting it, an approach that results in steadfastness in focus. They are also comfortable making decisions in light of ambiguity. Essentially, they can and want to obtain as

FIGURE 2-2

High-performing CIO thinking style

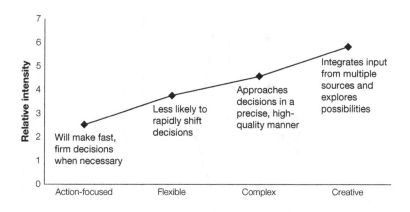

Source: Korn/Ferry International.

much information as possible, synthesizing multiple views of the same problem and arriving at a range of solutions.

That means that the most effective CIOs solicit input from a wide array of peers, subordinates, superiors, and external stakeholders (so you can see why their soft skills are so important) while also synthesizing inputs from the economy in general, company culture, technology industry, business industry, and societal trends, to create a broad set of solutions. From there, the CIOs choose what they consider the best solution and stick to it, until meaningful shifts in the data show a need to change.

As you can see in figure 2-3, the thinking tendencies of top performers differ significantly from those of lower performers. The relative emphasis on complex and creative thinking styles is much greater in the high-performing group. The thinking styles are more tightly bunched for the lower performers, who also tend to make greater use of the action-focused thinking style.

Figure 2-3 also illustrates how the high performers' thinking style evolves over time. Over the course of their career

FIGURE 2-3

Thinking styles by management level

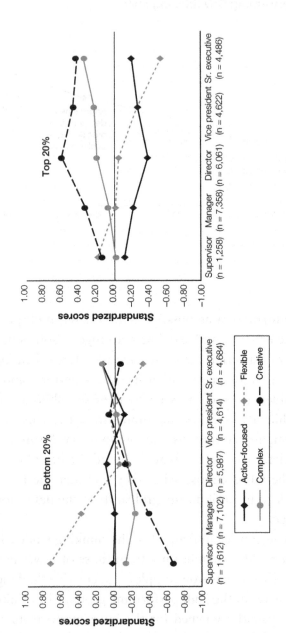

Source: Korn/Ferry International.

progression, the high performers' use of the complex and creative thinking styles steadily increases while the use of the action-focused and flexible thinking styles tapers off. In contrast, the low performers' thinking styles gradually "funnel" together into an undifferentiated mix.

Armed with this understanding on how the best CIOs think, let's move on to how they lead.

HIGH PERFORMERS: SOCIAL-PARTICIPATIVE LEADERS

Leadership style is how an executive creates a decision when in public or when he or she is conscious of being observed. Much like thinking styles, leadership styles differ by how people gather and use information and how they develop solutions. These styles also fall into four categories.

A *task-focused* leader uses clear, concise communications and states expectations explicitly and succinctly. The leader expresses views candidly and directly. He or she focuses on immediate tasks, driving for results and focusing on a single solution.

A *social* leader is approachable. He or she is always soliciting others' input and creates an environment that is informal and interactive. These leaders drive to create cross-functional relationships and use humor to ease tense situations. They are comfortable with many solutions to a single problem.

An *intellectual* leader relies on knowledge and expertise and has an inclination to stand firm. These kinds of leaders communicate detailed expectations and information. They drive for quality, focusing on a single, "best" solution.

A *participative* leader is collaborative and patient. He or she is open to alternate viewpoints and appreciates idea exchange. This leader encourages consensus and drives for inclusiveness. Like the intellectual leader, a participative leader is comfortable with using large amounts of information to reach a conclusion. But unlike the intellectual leader, he or she encourages that input from others and is willing to consider multiple options.

In action, the leadership pattern of the highest performers can be represented as in figure 2-4.

While all CIOs lead people using all four traits to some degree, the highest performers score in the upper range in the social and participative categories. These are key factors in their success. The converse also proves the point. The research shows that individuals who do not score well in these two categories are significantly hindered as they try to reach the most senior levels of the organization (figure 2-5).

The figure also illustrates that just as with thinking style, leadership style evolves over time. High performers start off their career more task-focused and intellectual in their leadership

FIGURE 2-4

High-performing CIO leadership style

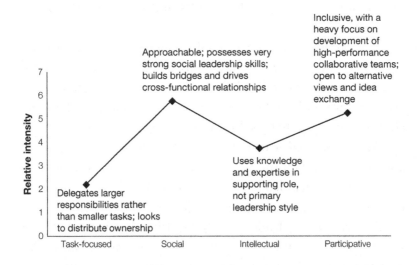

Source: Korn/Ferry International.

FIGURE 2-5

Leadership styles by management level

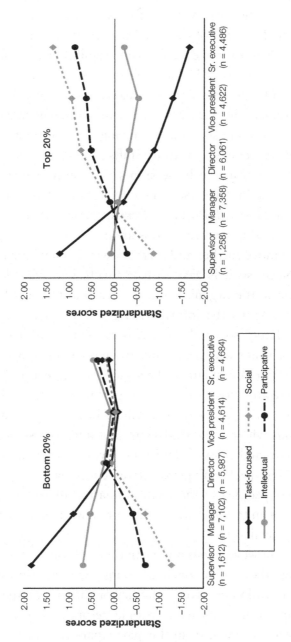

Source: Korn/Ferry International.

style, crossing over to the social-participative styles as they climb the org chart. Around the time of their first real management role, they experiment with all four styles equally. They quickly recognize the power of the social-participative styles, continuing to hone them over the years, while significantly reducing their use of the other two. Unlike their successful peers, the lower 20 percent of CIOs never deeply develop any one style as they move up the ranks. The way they lead seems to change like the wind. The result is confusion and a growing sense of frustration with the leader's seemingly arbitrary shifts in style.

This evolution in leadership style simply makes sense, as pointed out in "The Seasoned Executive's Decision-Making Style," a *Harvard Business Review* article that summarizes KFI's leadership research in this area: "As you move up the ladder, you move further and further away from where the action takes place, so it is easy to lose touch with what is actually going on in the organization. It's essential to use a leadership style that keeps the information pipeline open and the data flowing freely, so you have access to the best information and analysis. That's why the flexible [social] and integrative [participative] styles dominate at the senior executive level."[3]

There are a couple of other important aspects of the leadership style of high-performing CIOs. In meetings and external situations where these leaders are not under pressure, they are inquisitive and relaxed, and they involve others and listen to them. High-performing executives continually seek information from people as a means of evaluating alternative solutions and are open to integrating different views as new information becomes available.

This, however, does not mean they are constantly laid-back. Although they remain open and outgoing in high-pressure situations, they do not have the luxury of gathering large amounts of information from many people before acting. As a result, these leaders switch from this participative, inquisitive leadership style to a faster-paced social approach, which results in swifter action.

But in either situation, these executives demonstrate a very open style of leadership that helps them adapt and meet others on their terms. They are effective at team building; they are naturals at quickly developing social relationships. This ability enables the CIOs to achieve buy-in and commitment, rapidly adapt to new situations, build teams, and achieve results.

LEARNING TO THINK ONE WAY
AND LEAD ANOTHER

So where does that leave us? Right here: the best CIOs have a solid grounding in technology; they solve problems through eliciting a wide variety of data from many sources. They deal well with ambiguity, patiently and thoroughly vet new data before changing course, and, as a result, make superior decisions.

Given all the descriptors in the paragraph above, these CIOs are definitely capable of building the best mousetrap. So, it would be reasonable to assume that they would lead through pure intellectual power. After all, they are very often extremely smart, and it would be natural for them to try to lead by capitalizing on that strength.

And yet, when it comes time to move the group toward action, the most effective CIOs don't follow the intellect-focused route. While the best CIOs have a complex and creative decision-making style that is capable of producing very high-quality results, they lead through people, not through

---

The best CIOs have learned to lead not only far differently than they did when they were further down the organization chart, but also far differently than how they typically use their brain power. They rely on the social-participative styles that foster commitment to common goals, not pure intellect.

---

their expertise or superior brain power. In other words, *they think analytically but act collaboratively.*

Going back to our story with Stephen Fugale, if Stephen led the same way he thought, he would have announced the decision on the phone system after he completed his analysis and, when pressed, most likely would have argued why it was the best (i.e., the best technology, the best architecturally, at the best cost). While he may very well have been right, he would have implemented a system that lacked the support he would have gained by using a more participative style.

The CIO role is dense with challenging, politically charged, and otherwise complex decisions, where failure to garner the requisite support is a recipe for disaster. For example, when Pascal Buffard (CIO of Axa France) was challenged by his CEO to lead the integration effort following a major acquisition, the approach he took was pivotal to the ultimate success:

> Despite the aggressive time line, I knew I had to approach this decision in a way that the major stakeholders from both Axa and the acquired company could be involved in the choices. We put working groups of IT professionals in place with the mission to bring a recommendation to the executive committee in less than two months. I coached the IT guys to also actively manage the relationship with their respective executive committee members.[4]
>
> Fast-forward to the board meeting: the proposal was accepted, and we received a standing ovation. Why? Because we took the time to understand the most important motivations and priorities of each executive committee member. We spent the time—including over dinners and some late-night discussions—to make sure that they were included, to make them the sponsors of the choices made. It was not easy; some were from Axa, and some from the acquired company. But ultimately, it was very successful because it was not my proposal; it was the proposal of the executive committee members.

This approach laid the foundation for a successful and rapid integration. Partly as a result of this success, Buffard was promoted to chief operating officer and general secretary, adding to his CIO responsibilities of Axa France Services (processes and change management) and Axa France Support (administrative management, governance, legal, and audit).

With these examples in mind, consider figure 2-6, which overlays the two patterns of the highest-performing CIOs: their thinking style (figure 2-2) and their leading style (figure 2-4). You can actually see how the best CIOs think one way, yet lead another. Indeed, the gap between the social leadership style and the corresponding flexible thinking style is significant and meaningful (i.e., more than one point different), as is the gap between intellectual leadership and complex thinking.

Look at the "thinking" line in figure 2-6. You will see that these executives apparently reached a conclusion about how best to approach an issue, yet they purposefully pushed themselves to seek out others' input, never publicly suggesting they had come up with the answer. Rather, publicly, they are continuously

FIGURE 2-6

High-performing CIOs think analytically and act collaboratively

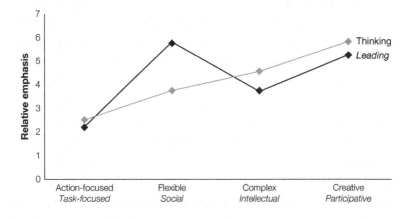

Source: Korn/Ferry International.

collaborating. In the end, what you most likely see is a solution similar to the one they came up with on their own. But now, the solution has been evolved to the point that it has the highest likelihood of being fully supported and properly valued.

To sum it all up, the highest-performing CIOs follow these practices:

- They do, in the words of the chapter title, lead very differently than they think. They have a highly social-participative leadership style, while having a highly complex and creative thinking style.

- They remain confident in difficult and complex situations without becoming egotistical, because of their ability to tolerate ambiguity and their willingness to call on the experience, smarts, insights, and passion of many others.

- They spend most of their time engaged in people activities: involving other people and building relationships up, down, and sideways both inside and outside the organization. (We will talk more about this in chapter 4.)

Why is all this so critical for you? That's simple. As we have said throughout, the only way to get work done is by, through, and with people. And people simply will not give you their best efforts if they feel coerced or cowed into taking a position because you have argued them into it. It doesn't really matter how compelling your argument is; people want to feel that they are part of the problem-solving and decision-making process, not as if they are just being given the solution to execute.

So the best CIOs lead through vision and involvement, using influence, not authority. They work hard to make sure the people they are leading have contributed to the idea—as Fugale did in the story that began the chapter—so these people feel that they own it. The CIOs have learned that this is the best way to lead.

As Beth Perlman, former chief administrative officer and, prior to that, CIO of Constellation Energy, said, "I have the intellectual horsepower, but I understood long ago that being smart didn't get me buy-in. Developing deep relationships did. After all, how can I lead with the best solution when most business executives aren't technology experts? At some point, they will have to take risks, given that they don't know everything about the technology, and they take those risks with me because I have created personal credibility with them."[5]

Here's how another high performer puts it: "I know I am the smartest person in the room when it comes to my domain, but I have come to learn that others in the room couldn't care less about my domain. They care about themselves and their success or failure within this business. I need to present my ideas in terms of what is in it for them."

Most CIOs we interviewed were able to cite a specific point in their career when they realized that as important as their technological knowledge is—and it is vital—they needed to be spending more time developing their people skills. In other words, they needed to lead differently than how they usually thought about things. For many, this "aha" moment came at the feet of a great mentor, someone who was already demonstrating the value of keen interpersonal skills and people leadership. For a smaller subset of high performers, the aha moment is more evolutionary. It doesn't matter how you get there, as long as you do, because the payoff for you can be huge.

DELIVERING RESULTS AND IT VALUE

As we have discussed, no matter how great your idea, how "perfect" the solution you have designed, it counts for nothing if others (particularly your business partners) do not share your enthusiasm or embrace and drive the change needed to realize the business benefits. Figure 2-7 shows how social and participative leadership and creative, complex thinking intersect with

FIGURE 2-7

Social-participative leadership skills enable collaborative delivery of business results

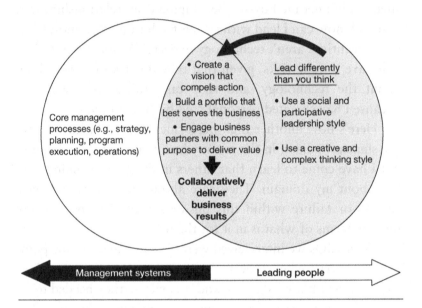

core IT management practices to unlock and amplify your ability as CIO to deliver business results and maximize IT value.

The CIO's skill as a social-participative leader turns key management practices, ones that all too often can be perceived as chores and lack effectiveness, into the underpinnings of superior business results. Specifically, CIOs can deliver results and maximize IT value because they *collaboratively accomplish* key outcomes.

- Create a vision that compels all to a common purpose and action, rather than one that becomes "shelfware" (i.e., something that just sits on a shelf forever, never to be looked at again).

- Build and fund a portfolio that best serves the entire business, as opposed to one that services the squeakiest wheel.

- Engage business partners, motivating them to action and a shared commitment to delivering results (i.e., assign the best people, as opposed to those "with time on their hands").

- Develop an organization that delivers on time and on budget and that can collaborate across boundaries to deliver needed business outcomes.

This all sounds good. But how do we know it is the right path to pursue? As figure 2-7 indicates, leading people in a social-participative style rather than intellectually means the difference between being frustrated with why others "do not get it" (or your great ideas do not get adopted, or you get marginalized or isolated) and being satisfied by making a difference, rallying others around great ideas, collaborating to make it happen, and ultimately delivering on the ideas and creating value.

Clearly, if you want to excel within the senior executive ranks, you need to lead differently than you think.

CALL TO ACTION

If you haven't yet learned to lead in a way that differs from your thinking style, consider the following tips:

PUT YOUR LEADERSHIP STYLE UNDER THE MICRO-SCOPE. Make your own graph depicting your leadership style, similar to the ones in the figures. Do the social-participative elements stand out from the others? Can you point to vivid examples of how you have applied them and made a difference? If the answers to those questions are no, then consider not only what you can do to elevate those aspects of your style, but also how you can scale back some of your reliance on the task-focused and intellectual styles.

ADD A THIRD LEG TO YOUR LEADERSHIP STOOL.
Strive to be as smart and skilled about people leadership as you
are about business and technology. Recognize that what got
you here won't get you there. Look to those who have already
made this transition, and determine what you can learn from
them. Enlist them as a trusted coach or mentor.

EMBRACE THE COUNTERINTUITIVE.   Part of leading is
letting go. To move ahead and become a more complete leader,
you need to shift a portion of your time and energy to developing strong people-leadership skills. That leaves less for the other
things. That's OK; your technical and business skills aren't going
anywhere. There will be plenty of opportunity to keep them
fresh and honed. They just can't be your dominant focus any
longer.

BREAK OUT OF YOUR COMFORT ZONE.   Open yourself
up to recognizing and learning new ways of doing things as a
leader. This may be a bit scary at first, and your efforts will
definitely not always meet with success on the first try, but that's
fine. As you know, we often learn more from our failures and
mishaps then we do from our successes. Then look for opportunities to apply the learning you have gained to fresh challenges.

ASK, WHAT IF?   For example, what might you have accomplished (or how much easier might it have been accomplished) if
you had applied strong social-participative skills to a challenge?
Reflective (and forward-looking) questions like these will help
you break out of your current mode of thinking about leadership and help you to recognize opportunities for applying your
newly developed leadership skills.

SUMMING UP

There is absolutely no doubt that mastering the additional five people-leadership skills that we will discuss in chapters 3 through 7 is vital to your success as a CIO. But if you try to learn them in a vacuum, you will be missing out. Those skills flow from a different way of leading and relating—one that, as we have just seen, is different from the way the best CIOs think. They don't lead successfully by having developed the best mousetrap. And they don't lead through pure intellectual horsepower. They lead by a social-participative style, by developing the best people relationships. For most successful CIOs, this is something they learned and evolved over time. If you want to be among the best, you need to make the transition now and hone your social-participative leadership style.

EMBRACE YOUR SOFTER SIDE . . .

(AND MOVE FROM GOOD TO GREAT AS A RESULT)

The CIO of a Fortune 200 company, who asked us not to use his name for reasons that will become clear in a minute, headed one of the highest-performing IT organizations by any objective standpoint. All the data showed that his department did the most with the least and had solid end-user customer satisfaction numbers.

Yet the CIO, let's call him John, was perplexed by having both his reporting relationship suddenly changed—he went from working directly for the CEO to answering to someone theoretically his peer on the org chart—and suboptimal support for his department. He just couldn't get the resources he needed, and he knew the perception of his department was far less than the reality he was producing.

John couldn't understand it. He had focused much of his time on the development of the IT organization—its competencies and morale—and had done so successfully. Indeed, his CEO told us that he felt the IT department was better at marketing and creating brand loyalty within its department than his marketers were in presenting the company's image to the world. And yet both John and his department were seen as second-class citizens.

Faced with this disconnect, John decided to be formally assessed and participated in an externally facilitated 360-degree review. The results: John received extremely high marks for the way he ran the department. But his empathy with colleagues wasn't nearly as high. His communication skills with his counterparts were also lacking. He certainly wasn't a bad communicator, as was clear from his impact on his own organization. Yet, he just didn't connect with his peers outside the department. They never quite grasped what he was talking about, what the IT department had accomplished, and—more importantly—how John's accomplishments could benefit them.

In short, after his assessment, John hired an executive coach and dedicated himself to understanding the nuances of his business peers—how they took in information, how they made decisions, and how they viewed themselves. Then he customized his communications with each person.

A lot of work? You bet. But John knew it had to be done. Otherwise, nothing would change. He knew he had to focus on "the people thing," and the people in this case were not his direct reports, but his colleagues within the organization.

Fast-forward twelve months. Not only is John back reporting to the CEO, but he has also been promoted and given responsibility over business operations along with IT.

JOHN'S STORY ILLUSTRATES a definitive pattern we found in observing CIOs. The people we talked to could be divided into three broad categories. There were some—the lowest performers—who were in trouble. They couldn't handle the day-to-day demands of the job, and their management skills were lacking. As a result of both flaws, they were looked down upon by members of the C-suite. At the other extreme were the high-performing CIOs, the ones we have featured throughout, the leaders who are simply exemplary.

And there was this huge middle group, people like John (before he decided to change). With apologies to Jim Collins, we would describe them as good, but not great. They had the necessary technical skills, were OK as managers, and got along with other stakeholders. But no one would hold the department up as a model of how things should be done, and these executives were perpetually frustrated and exhausted by all the things they had to do, the fires they had to put out, and the mismatched expectations with their colleagues.

At first we thought the difference between the middle group and the top performers was people skills—and we were partly right. But it's not that the middle group has terrible people skills; they don't. As John's story shows, they understand—at least intellectually—the importance of inspiring people, communicating effectively, building relationships, and concentrating more on building people (as opposed to systems), all topics that we will deal with at length in subsequent chapters. However, as we dug a little deeper, we noticed that these CIOs didn't truly embrace those things to a point where it guides the way they lead every day.

This is an important distinction. While everyone understands why people skills are vital, the best CIOs raise those skills to another level. They are simply exemplary at relating to people and making connections.

An amazing power is unleashed when you create a connection. Standing in isolation, the most powerful computer in the world is just a mess of useless wires and silicon. Connect it to a power source and the World Wide Web, and what you can do is virtually limitless. It's no different when we are talking about people, especially when we are discussing what happens at work. On our own, there are limits to what we can accomplish alone as managers. But put us in a high-functioning relationship or on a terrific team, and the connections we can create allow us to do awe-inspiring work.

A POTENTIALLY TROUBLING QUESTION

Are your "soft skills" and your ability to make connections with people as well honed as your technological savvy and business acumen? Do they even come close? Are they impairing your ability to lead?

The best CIOs forge those connections and tap into deeply rooted, human emotional drivers to unleash the incredibly powerful force of energized people. A key element in the way they do this is demonstrating that they care, and relating to those around them—not only their direct reports but their colleagues outside the department, the CEO and the board, and all of the organization's stakeholders.

Having real relationships with these people allows you to cut through all the politics and other nonsense surrounding an issue and quickly get to the heart of the matter, so that you can reach a collaborative and informed decision. This is why, after you've committed to being a people leader first and to thinking one way while leading another, the next step in becoming a great CIO is to fully embrace the soft, interpersonal skills that can create a high-energy connection with others.

This chapter will highlight the three particular competencies that are essential to forming a deep, meaningful connection with others: (1) being open and receptive, (2) caring, and (3) relating. As shown in figure 3-1, the more open, receptive, caring, and relating a CIO is, the better his or her communications, relationships, and ability to inspire. That, in turn, positively affects the value the IT department can add organizationwide.

These competencies of openness, a caring attitude, and relating well to others lay a critical foundation for the CIO as a people-oriented leader. They can also enable and enhance the other critical soft skills we highlight in chapters 4 through 7 (managing diverse relationships, communicating with people, inspiring them, and developing them).

FIGURE 3-1

Soft skills yield hard results

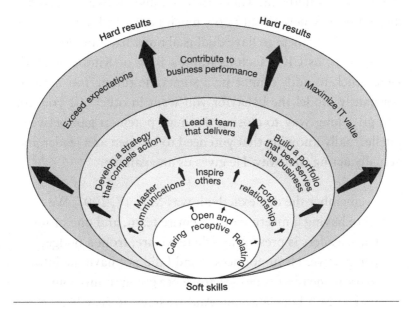

Some detail will bring all this to life. Before we begin, please note that when we discuss the specific competencies featured in this chapter and throughout the remainder of the book, we will be using terminology associated with the Leadership Architect, the library of competencies developed by KFI's Lominger International. We chose the Lominger framework because it is familiar to many executives, has been heavily researched, and is easily applied for leadership development purposes. With that by way of background, let's move on to the first of three competencies in this chapter.

BEING OPEN AND RECEPTIVE

Intriguingly, we heard a consistent theme from the high performers whom we interviewed—a key part of embracing your softer side is to open up yourself. As Carol J. Zierhoffer, vice president and CIO for ITT's Information Technology Sector, puts it,

"When I reveal not only who I am, but what I am, and why I am, it's very hard for those on the other side of the relationship to doubt my commitment. They might not always like a decision I make, but they never doubt how much I care, and that makes it even harder for them to have doubts about what I am doing."[1]

But this, as CIOs such as Ramón Baez of Kimberly-Clark were quick to add, cannot be a sometime thing. You need to constantly model the behavior you want in others. If you do, you go a long way to closing the huge potential gap between intellectually knowing that you need to be open as a leader and actually acting that way. He gives us an example:

> I remember the day exactly; it was May 17, 2007. We were having a meeting of the entire team, and one of my team leaders is presenting where we are, from a budget perspective. He announces—and I did not have the information ahead of time—that we are going to miss our budget by a huge amount. And we have no easy fix. We just messed up on our budget.
>
> When I heard that, I could have gotten really mad—and believe me, that was my first, second, and third reaction. But what I said to myself was that the worst thing I can do is explode, because it will create a situation where people start saying, "Don't ever bring bad news to Ramón, because he's just going to rip your head off in front of everybody." That's what was going through my head.
>
> So I told the group, "Listen, there's nothing we're going to be able to do about that right this minute. Let's continue getting through this meeting, and then we'll talk about what are the next steps on how to get this thing corrected."
>
> And because I remained calm and cool and collected there—and I'm going to tell you, I'm not like that every time—everyone wanted to help. Everyone wanted to be part of the solution in fixing that problem. Even more important to me than solving the immediate problem was

that as a leader, I role-modeled a culture of openness—one where I was approachable and people were not afraid to surface bad news.[2]

How do you demonstrate this kind of openness, in practice? The best CIOs do it by engaging in active listening, demonstrating vulnerability, and using humor when appropriate. We'll explain all three.

Listen Actively

Active listeners pay rapt attention to what is being communicated to them through both words and nonverbal cues such as body language and facial expressions. They also have a thirst for real feedback. Even when the response is extremely critical of what they are doing, they do not rationalize it away or dismiss what others say.

This active listening is not always easy, as one CIO told us: "I always thought I had really solid interpersonal skills until I had one of my first 360s as a CIO. I got rave remarks on my listening skills, but not from everyone. It turned out I was a selective listener. I turned it on and off, depending on whom I was speaking with. Now I listen patiently—and sometimes it's hard work—to everyone. The payoff is that I know so much more about things and I am able to be more proactive."

Demonstrate Vulnerability

Vulnerability usually doesn't make the short list of characteristics that most would identify with great leadership. However, when applied correctly, it has a profound impact and can be used to the leader's advantage.

A particularly effective way to demonstrate vulnerability is through the use of personal disclosure. As a case in point, we found the CIOs we spoke with to be incredibly self-aware and not concerned about sharing what flows out of that awareness. They know their strengths and weaknesses and engage in honest conversations about how to best use both. They have become comfortable with not only what to disclose, but also how people's personal lives and office lives can work hand-in-hand. They know that talking about their personal experiences—that they had a family emergency (their eleven-year-old broke her arm) or how hard they had to work to learn to overcome their anxiety of speaking in public—makes them more human and approachable.

Successful CIOs show they care enough about the people they work with to make themselves vulnerable so that it can be a truly two-way relationship. In other words, by demonstrating vulnerability—hoping that others will open themselves up in return—these CIOs are creating an environment that supports openness and sets the stage for stronger relationships.

Use Humor

These great CIOs have an ability to work through difficult situations not just with listening, but also with humor—often at their own expense. In interviewing peers and subordinates of Tom Tabor, senior vice president and CIO of Highmark, a major health insurer, to find out why he was so successful, we found one obvious theme: his use of self-deprecating humor. "He's not the most comfortable speaker, and he really doesn't like conflict, but he gets movement because he knows just how and when to make a joke at his own expense that releases all the tension in the room," one of his direct reports told us.

What's also unique about these high performers is they rarely engage in negative humor, such as being sarcastic, as a

---

Are you willing to accept that it is only by opening up and becoming more vulnerable that you can achieve the people connectedness you need to inspire the right people to get the right things done?

---

means to deliver a negative message. "I've experienced how draining a sarcastic leader can be, and I don't want that for my people," said one CIO we interviewed. "I want to be the person that can ease the tension in a room through laughter, but not at someone else's expense."

CARING

Not only do CIOs show, in all the ways you would expect, that they care about the people they work with, but they are also fair—to everyone. Yes, of course, top performers are given more challenging assignments, greater responsibilities, and larger paychecks if they accomplish their goals. But everyone is held to the same standards (i.e., they are expected to act ethically and do their job well) and has the opportunity to grow according to demonstrated performance.

In talking about his boss, one midlevel manager we interviewed said, "It's easy to be fair to the high performers. But what's harder, is that he is fair to those that weren't pulling their weight. He didn't let them slide, but provided them a picture of the future, how they needed to fit in, and created performance plans to get them there. He is willing to have difficult conversations with them as well. He gives everyone the ability to see what needs to be done and the opportunity to demonstrate they can do it."

As a result of being fair and caring, high-performing CIOs engender a deep sense of loyalty and "followership," even when tough people decisions are called for.

RELATING

The top CIOs are approachable and relate well to others. Let's take each point separately.

Approachable. They are sensitive to, and patient with, the anxieties, concerns, fears, hopes, dreams, and aspirations of others. These executives work hard—by both listening well and asking open-ended questions to discover what is going on early in the process so that they have time to shape outcomes, instead of just reacting.

Obviously, if you are arrogant, judgmental, or simply oblivious, people are going to be reluctant to approach you. As Ross Philo, CIO of the U.S. Postal Service, says, "one of the challenges when you're in a senior role is that people tend to be intimidated by the title or the position. I work hard to bring interactions down to a much more human scale if I possibly can. I try to engage. Show enthusiasm. I always try to be upbeat and optimistic. And I try not to allow external pressures or pressures from above to be transmitted to my team."[3]

Adept at relating well to all kinds of people at all levels. Top business leaders do this through focusing on others first, not the agenda at hand. Someone in the C-suite said this about the company's CIO: "He's not a pushover. He stands toe to toe when he needs to. But he understands when he needs to change tactics, because he's taken the time and patience to understand the situation and the people involved." This relating is paramount to business partners and other colleagues. The best CIOs can empathize with their partners' situation, pressures, trade-offs, and challenges. But whether they are dealing with people inside the organization or outside it, the ability to relate fosters a bond, a common understanding and platform for collaborative partnership and working through tough issues.

The takeaway from all this is clear: the best CIOs spend the time to know not only themselves but also others. Then, through their deep respect for everyone and their recognition that everyone is different, these leaders create deep, personal bonds with people to enable trusted, collaborative decision processes and relationships.

SOFTNESS DOESN'T PRECLUDE TOUGHNESS

Let's stop here. This is not just soft and squishy stuff that we are talking about. These soft skills *are not* replacing all the tough, hard responsibilities a leader has—setting high expectations and holding people to them; working through difficult decisions with business partners; delivering projects on time and on budget; and the like. The best CIOs do that. (In fact, they hold themselves and everyone else to higher standards.) *So these soft skills are not replacing all those things, but augmenting them.*

But, intriguingly, forging deep connections—the soft stuff—makes the rest of the job easier and provides the foundation for superior performance. These kinds of connections create tangible results. The CIOs who employ them get the most out of people and out of their roles as CIOs.

Look at any of the organizations we've highlighted, and you will find IT departments that are the most tightly aligned with business requirements; IT organizations that don't have problems attracting the best talent; CIOs who spend the most time with CEOs and board members . . . and the list goes on.

Consider what Duffy Mees, CIO of Promontory Interfinancial Network (PIN), accomplished when he was at Independence Air. He created the entire IT infrastructure—everything from how passengers and travel agents would make reservations and receive tickets, to how corporate employees would get paid—in nine months.

But as Mees is quick to point out, he had two advantages. First, he knew how the big carriers handled IT. While working at a regional carrier that connected to major airlines, he had seen firsthand all the inherent problems in the airlines' IT departments—multiple legacy systems that had trouble talking to one another, everything handled on mainframes, etc.—so he knew what to avoid.

And second, he knew he could enlist a group of people to accomplish the seemingly impossible: getting an airline off the ground in nine months, when three years would have been the norm.

> I got my team together, and we agreed that we were not going to commit the sins of the past. We knew everything not to do. So we sat down and said, "All right, what does IT for Independence Air need to look like?" And we decided it had to be simple, reliable, and scalable and provide a significant return on investment. And those four attributes would govern everything that we did.
>
> We built an infrastructure that could be supported by as few as twenty IT people, even though we were serving forty-six cities nationwide. We looked at technologies that we could deploy and that would eliminate the need to travel to fix something. We wanted to support everything centrally from our data center. All and all, we created a simple, elegant design and something that was very fast and easy to manage and monitor. Plus, it was heavily automated. A lot of times, IT focuses so much on providing automation to the end users, that they don't have any internally. Everything is manual. That was one of the reasons why it took 186 of their people to run their airline, where I could do it with 20.[4]

As impressive as all that is, Mees says that it's the way he began the explanation—"I got my team together"—that was actually the most important.

> One of the corporate mandates was making flying faster and easier for our customers. All of our technology had to contribute to that, and so we'd actually go out to the business and stand behind them at the ticket counters and

the gates and watch them process passengers. Anything that took more than fifteen seconds, we'd go find a way to automate it. I was out at the airport just as much as any of my people, and I think that's one of the important attributes of a good CIO. Yeah, you've got to elevate yourself up to the level of CIO, but you can't lose touch with the frontline people so that you can provide support to them and the guidance and mentoring and leadership that they need. And if you're not in touch with the front line, I don't know how you can do that.

I think when people see their leader is someone who cares about them, who creates an environment where mistakes are expected and learned from, then they just work better. I remember being very honest with the team about my personal fears. We talked often that my greatest love of being a CIO wasn't the technology, but the impact. But I also shared with them how hard it is sometimes to work tirelessly on something and being insecure that the business really understood what you were doing for them.

So I had my doubts; we all did. But we talked about them. I remember keeping an open door. I really wanted them to feel I cared and I was in this with them as much as they were. Sometimes I think I had more people in my office commiserating or problem solving than we had out on the floor. I remember we would routinely have meetings and everybody would say, "Nobody knows how hard it is to deliver what these people are asking for, because we're kind of our own worst enemy because we always deliver. We've never, ever failed the company."

And I said, "I know, but that's the curse of being in IT." Well, on my very last day at Independence Air, Kerry Skeen, the CEO, called me into his office, and he said, "Hey, listen, I just wanted you to know, I never had the opportunity to tell you this, but through all these years, in all of the negotiations and the business opportunities that we had, we always considered IT to be our ace in the hole, and I don't know any other company that can say that. We know we asked ridiculous things of you, and you always delivered." That was one of the most rewarding days of my career.

Mees's story is typical among the high performers we interviewed. Consider these other highly effective CIOs:

- Tim Zoph, CIO and senior vice president of Northwestern Memorial Hospital, who inherited an IT department at Northwestern with abnormally high turnover compared with the rest of organization, strongly believes that soft skills yield hard results. He applied everything we have talked about here, and turnover fell from 15 to 4 percent.

- Through his focus on people first, Richard Gius, when at Allegiance Healthcare, was able, in parallel, to utilize both on-shoring and off-shoring outsourcing arrangements to provide effective systems support and software development at lower IT costs than using in-house resources. He did that while simultaneously creating a more flexible, variable work force to project related/new functionality development work.

- Thanks to his people skills, which we will see in action a little bit later, Dave Swartz, the CIO of American University, received a double-digit increase in his budget during the recent recession (while other universities' budgets were being cut).

These were not onetime things. They are sustainable results. To find out what makes them sustainable, we must take a quick step backward.

As you will recall from the earlier chapters, the best CIOs don't just create a vision; they create a vision that compels action: one that builds and funds a portfolio that best serves the business, engages business partners, and motivates them to action.

The CIOs who have fully embraced their softer side make
deep connections and energize the people around them. They
consequently get more done with less and are tightly aligned
with internal partners and outside stakeholders alike.

BETTER INFORMATION, NO SURPRISES

As we engaged in a series of events, meetings, and interviews
with CIOs across the United States, we talked to them about
the initial set of conclusions we had drawn from our first round
of research, and as we did, we had another "aha" moment.
Not only are the best CIOs dedicated to creating deep, personal
relationships, but these relationships actually allowed leaders
to anticipate (and ultimately help shape) the future.

When CIOs were able to develop a high degree of connectedness, they found they had a real ability to be proactive, something they repeatedly told us was important. We heard over
and over about the importance of *sensing* changes in the needs
of the business. Yes, the CIOs were all members of organizations that had regular project prioritization meetings; strategy,
planning, and budgeting processes; and the like. But what the
deep relationships with peers brought them was a real sense of
what was changing, how it was changing, and, most importantly, why it was changing. And they learned this long before
the formal meetings to discuss priorities. It was as if an old
cliché had come to life.

We have all heard that there is no such thing as a crisis;
we only have opportunities. Well, that is only true if we have
adequate time to respond to the looming problem. At some
point, problems do, indeed, grow into crisis, if you don't do
anything about them.

But what the CIOs with superior interpersonal skills were
telling us was because of the relationships they had formed,

they got more and better information earlier, which gave them a chance to respond and shape the future, instead of simply reacting to it. They could *collaboratively* intervene in time, using their interpersonal skills to make sure that everyone walked away from the intervention understanding exactly what the problem was—"this project is going off the rails because of A, B, and C"—as opposed to thinking that "the CIO is just a barrier and just doesn't understand."

As a result of having in place relationships that significantly improved the information flow and allowed them to know what was truly going on, these CIOs said they had an ability to better manage their own staffs and budgets to adjust for the change. The result: a continually aligned IT department that could respond faster and better to the needs of the organization, thereby truly helping to shape the future of the enterprise. This amplification effect is depicted in figure 3-2.

FIGURE 3-2

The amplification effect: Embracing your softer side improves information flow and maximizes business results

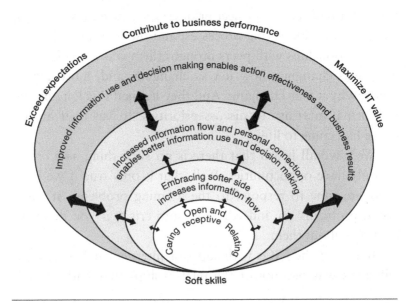

THE PROBLEM WITH COMMAND
AND CONTROL

We have said throughout that soft skills yield hard results. And this chapter certainly illustrates how CIOs' ability to establish deep, personal connections with those around them is the foundation to move from good to great. We also, however, sometimes hear the voices of skeptics. They tend to drive results through pure command and control and by being a harsh task master. This is not the style we saw in the high-performing leaders. When we asked why, they answered that you can "muscle" results or "intimidate" to gain results up to a point, but it is never as powerful or sustainable as having energized, motivated people. Eventually, all those people you browbeat are going to quit, find another job, become resentful (and do the absolute minimum at best or sabotage the efforts of the company at worst), or simply burn out.

FIGURE 3-3

Embracing your soft side creates a connectedness that fully engages everyone in driving results

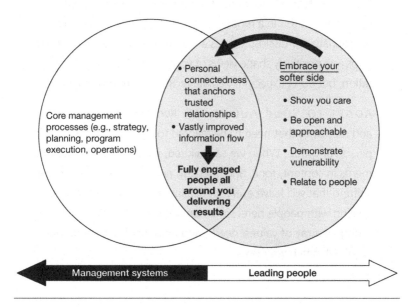

As we have said throughout, a key emotional driver for energized, motivated people is that they feel you care; they can relate to you; that their voice is heard and their contribution is recognized. You can see that payoff in figure 3-3.

The payoff from successfully tapping into these emotional drivers can be immense, but the downside from ignoring them has an equal impact!

CALL TO ACTION

If your soft skills still have some noticeably rough edges, consider the following development suggestions:

PRACTICE THE FIRST RULE OF LISTENING. Ask questions. Not just any questions. Ask probing, open-ended questions, ones that reveal more quickly and clearly what your audience is really trying to tell you. These types of questions begin with *How?* and *Why?* They do wonders to stimulate dialogue and get to a deeper, shared understanding.

BE WILLING TO MAKE YOURSELF VULNERABLE. Start small. No need to go right out there and reveal any whoppers (more on this in a moment). A little bit of well-timed and appropriate self-disclosure goes a long way to strengthen relationships and positively shape views of your leadership. Invite collaboration, but don't expect immediate reciprocation. Give it time.

ADAPT TO YOUR AUDIENCE. Recognize the behaviors and messages that need to be tailored to connect with a specific person or group. When we say tailored, we mean subtle adjustments in content, tone, and intensity, not chameleon-like shape shifting that will leave everyone feeling a bit confused. You are dealing with people here, so remember that you will be encountering an array of values, needs, and emotional styles and they won't all match your own.

WHAT ARE YOUR FIRST WORDS? As a senior leader, you make an immediate, high-impact impression on others. Your first move in an interaction will have a strong influence on what path that interaction heads down. So, monitor closely your first words and how others initially respond to them. Don't forget body language, too. (We will be talking more about this in chapter 5, "Master Communications.")

RESPECT BOUNDARIES. In an effort to more fully embrace your softer side, be careful not to overcompensate. Be particularly mindful of when you engage in open disclosure (there is a time and a place for everything, so choose the right moment and setting) and what you relate. People have varying comfort zones, so test them carefully. If possible, take a cue from what they seem comfortable sharing.

SUMMING UP

The best CIOs do, indeed, embrace their softer side. They do it in order to form deep, personal connections with not only their direct reports, but also their peers, the CEO, the board, and other key stakeholders.

What allows them to do it, and why do they do so? They can embrace their softer side because they have deeply honed interpersonal skills that they combine with a vulnerability. A leader's vulnerability tells those on the other side of the table—or on the other end of the phone, e-mail, or document—that they are dealing with a real, authentic person, one who believes what he or she is saying and can be trusted.

Why do top performers open themselves up this way? Allowing vulnerability builds trust and a personal connection at a far deeper, interpersonal level. This in turn motivates the people the CIO is interacting with to contribute their best work, invites greater performance, and supports the achievement of extraordinary results.

What's more, it allows both the CIO and all the people he or she comes in contact with to move more quickly and easily beyond the superficial and political concerns surrounding an issue. In this way, they can collaboratively find the very best solution (and do so early, since the relationships they have in place allow them to get information from informal, as well as formal, channels). The net result is people who are more energized, relationships that are more aligned, decisions that are more collaborative and informed, and an environment where IT can both operate at a higher level and provide maximum value.

FORGE RIGHT RELATIONSHIPS, DRIVE RIGHT RESULTS

GO SIDEWAYS TO MOVE AHEAD

Robert Runcie, chief administrative officer and formerly CIO of the Chicago Board of Education, the nation's third-largest public school system (409,000 students, 43,700 employees, and an annual budget of $5.3 billion in fiscal year 2010), is talking about relationships.

> *One of the first things you realize is that there are some people who, while not the highest on the organization chart, have influence over everybody. That was the case with one high school principal, who, when I first encountered him, could only be described as my arch-enemy.*
>
> *I met him after I had been in the job for about a year and just gotten my head around a huge problem. My department was absorbing the cost of maintaining all the personal computers in the system, and the number*

of computers was soaring. Over a three-year period, we went from fifty thousand to almost a hundred and fifty thousand PCs. The schools bought them, but the expense of maintaining the machines, keeping them connected to the network, and making sure they had the appropriate filters and virus protection was coming out of my budget.

So I instituted a fee of $24 a year per machine that every school had to pay for every computer they had. Not surprisingly, it did not go over well.

I held several meetings with the principals to talk about it. And at one, where my boss was present, this one guy got up and he just starts screaming at me, saying I was stealing money from the schools. Then he called every principal he knew—and he knew just about all of them—and got them to agree they weren't going to pay the fee. And then he called the papers, and suddenly, this was a big, citywide story.

By this point, I figured I had nothing to lose. My relationship with him couldn't get any worse. So I called him and said, "I am putting together a couple of advisory committees because I really want to hear what you and the other school administrators are saying, so that we can improve what we're doing and make sure that our work is addressing your needs. I want you to help me to get better. Will you serve on one of my committees?"

He agreed, so I began to have a lot of conversations with him. I would call him occasionally to ask his advice about how I should approach this guy or to see what he thought about an idea I had.

It was just remarkable what happened after about six months. I was attending the monthly meeting of the Chicago Principals Association. One of the issues on the agenda concerned another department that had built a software application that we advised them not to do. It blew up and was a major fiasco. My department had

*nothing to do with it, but my name was on the agenda
item, because apparently anything that touches a computer
is my responsibility.*

*The president of the association starts the meeting
by saying, "We are ready to talk about Bob's disaster,"
and the principal who had hated me interrupts and says,
"Let's just stop here. I'm tired of you guys blaming Bob
and IT for stuff like this, which is not their fault. They
are doing a really good job. The problem is, you've got
a bunch of renegade departments out there not listening
to their advice."*

*He just went on a tirade defending us. It was almost
embarrassing. His comments at the meeting proved to me
the importance of relationships. When you find individuals who are difficult, you need to figure out how you can
collaborate and get close to them so you can get them
to really understand what it is you're trying to do.*

*I've made that my mantra every since. It really
works.*[1]

HIGH-PERFORMING PERSON-TO-PERSON relationships
deliver results for high-performing CIOs. The best CIOs
understand that soft skills and a social and participative style
are the keys to fostering high-performing relationships.

On one level, that finding—which jumped out from our
interviews and research—didn't surprise us. As we detailed in
chapter 2, the best-performing CIOs have a social and participative leadership style, one that naturally engages others. And
since, as we have seen, the only way to get work done today is
with others, we would have expected that the CIOs who formed
the best relationships would be the most successful. But what
did surprise us was that the highest-performing CIOs spent a
greater percentage of their time and energy managing relationships that exist sideways: with internal peers, with external
suppliers, with company customers.

You need to leverage your relationships in *all* directions. The strength of these relationships, especially the sideways ones, can quickly escalate to a "make or break" level, determining whether a CIO can meet expectations and maximize value delivery—or not. Not only is this critical now, but it will become increasing true as the hyperconnnected enterprise, which we discussed in chapter 1, becomes more commonplace and more firmly entrenched. Tomorrow's successful CIOs will need to deal with the dramatically increasing diversity (and hence complexity) of relationships both inside and outside the organization.

Let's show how all this plays in practice. We will start with the area where the highest-performing CIOs get the most leverage from their relationships—by concentrating on the horizontal ones. Next, we will talk about the all-important CIO-CEO relationship and will then describe the essential aspects of any relationship. And finally, we will discuss why you need to hone your political skills. (We cover the topic of developing your own team and the relationships within in chapter 7, "Build People, Not Systems.")

HORIZONTAL RELATIONSHIPS:
PROSPER OR PERISH

Like many CEOs of health-care organizations, Dean Harrison, of Northwestern Memorial in Chicago, first sets out to ensure complete alignment of any initiative with the organization's "Patients First" mission. One such project was to improve the way his hospital advanced patient care and maintained its patient records: "We implemented electronic medical records early in the adoption curve because it was the right thing to do for our patients; we could deliver more cost-effective, appropriate, evidence-based care as a result of this technology." Understanding how important and complex the investment in this technology would be—it called for infusing technology at the very heart of the patient care delivery process—he paired his chief nurse with his CIO to ensure the project was jointly designed and successfully implemented from the beginning.

As is the case with so many horizontal collaborations involving the CIO, the strength of the relationship is critical. As Harrison described, "When the chief nurse agreed to take on that new role and was paired with the CIO, they both were uncertain about how this new collaboration would work and who was in charge." Looking back, Harrison reflected to us:

> I was proud to watch two people, with distinctly different areas of responsibility, who had never worked together in this way before, effectively collaborate and accomplish this complex goal. Those are the traits that I am looking for in my key leaders. Each person is an expert in his or her own expertise and skills. I don't expect our CFO to be as knowledgeable about technology, as an example, as I would our CIO. What I do expect is that our team will work together in complementary ways to advance our vision.
>
> The two of them did the most fabulous job. Planning meetings focused on how to use technology as a tool and enabler for the business outcome that we were striving to achieve for our patients. Traditional work silos disappeared, therefore allowing a very successful implementation.[2]

Harrison's conclusion: "Relationships absolutely drive results."

A POTENTIAL TROUBLING QUESTION

What gets a CIO fired? We observe all too frequently it is the failure to build effective peer relationships, far more often than it is having a lackluster relationship with the CEO.

Are your relationships another asset, or a cause for concern?

Despite knowing how important horizontal relationships are, many CIOs we observed still gave them insufficient time and attention (typically being all consumed by management activities and by knocking off all the things on their to-do list) and consequently found themselves swept out of a job by this powerful force. As Carol Zierhoffer, CIO of ITT, says, relationships with peers can be either a tail wind or a headwind."[3]

To avoid facing headwinds, David Swartz, CIO of American University, has made it a practice in his last three jobs to create excellent sideways relationships. "There is always a power base that needs to be discovered, one that's usually not on the organization chart, and I have to focus on forging relationships with each member of that base." Those people fall into two broad categories: those who want to constantly improve the organization, and those who, as Swartz puts it, "have too much time on their hands and are always complaining about IT."

Swartz describes the importance of forming relationships with the "power base":

> If you spend some time, you can figure out who are the
> people I call the "thought leaders," the men and women
> most people in the organization follow. In our case, it
> is a handful of professors. They are the people who drive
> change here or can help prevent it. At each university
> where I have been a CIO, I have had to figure out who
> they are, and then start building relationships with them.[4]

Obviously, this is far from easy. As Steve Stone, Lowe's CIO, is quick to stress, "horizontal business relationships are the hardest to manage and the most time-consuming."[5] And yet you absolutely have to put in the effort.

We often witnessed the negative fallout from not spending enough time and energy. One common occurrence is when a critical change (either in process or in culture) needs to be implemented by the business to maximize the investment made in technology. The change doesn't matter. What matters is that the

CIO, working with the CEO and other functional executives, would gain support for what he or she wanted to do.

However, in the execution of that change, pushback from someone interrupts the process, and suddenly the CIO doesn't sense the full support at the C level that he thought he had. When you peel back the onion, it wasn't that the CEO had withdrawn support. It turns out that the top executive was stepping back to make sure that the CIO "did the homework" and created a true working relationship with the person pushing back on the implementation. The CEO had more important things to do than referee the fight between department heads.

The other common occurrence is when the use of an intellectual leadership style exposes the CIO's relationship shortcomings. In this instance, the CIO counts on gaining support by elegantly laying out arguments for the "optimal solution," rather than spending the appropriate up-front time developing a relationship based on trust and respect, one that is maintained continually, not just when needed.

It is worth expanding on that last sentence just a bit. No matter how good you are at your job, and no matter how wonderful the company you work for is, there are always going to be bumps in the road as you try to get things done. If you have a good personal and professional relationship with the people you work with, it will be easier to resolve the issue at hand. But this means, of course, that you need to have the relationship in place long before the problem pops up, because as Zierhoffer points out, "by the time you need a relationship, it is too late to develop it."

One reason that forming and maintaining these relationships is so hard is that, as we have seen, those sideways relationships often exist outside reporting lines. Swartz and the influential professors work in completely separate departments. Similarly, while the high school principal, like Runcie, was employed by the Chicago Board of Education, he didn't work for Runcie. In these (common) situations, the only way you can gain the cooperation, let alone support, you need is by forging deep, personal relationships.

QUICK QUIZ

List the three most influential direct reports to your CEO, the three most influential business people lower in your enterprise, and the three most influential external stakeholders. From each of their perspectives, how would they describe their relationship with you? In which relationships do you need to invest more time and attention?

For example, Runcie helped create that connection by utilizing the interpersonal skills we described in chapter 3, being open ("I really want to improve what we're doing and make sure that our work is addressing your needs"), receptive ("I really want to hear what you are saying"), and vulnerable ("I want you to help me to get better").

The Runcie story is instructive for another reason. It shows that winning relationships are built on a foundation of trust and authenticity. (So it is no wonder, then, that the best CIOs score so highly when it comes to such things as relating well and caring.) One of the reasons Runcie's former "arch-enemy" didn't trust him initially was because they had no relationship. Runcie imposed the $24 fee unilaterally. But once they had built up a relationship over time, the principal became an ally. Working on his soft skills ultimately produced hard results for Runcie.

SIDEWAYS RELATIONSHIPS

What is striking about managing sideways is the amount of lift it gives the CIOs who engage in it. By developing deep and open relationships, being vulnerable, welcoming suggestions, and being transparent, these CIOs create an atmosphere that invites involvement from their peers and leads to healthy collaboration.

WHY YOU NEED TO MANAGE SIDEWAYS

After conducting scores of CIO interviews, we felt certain that managing sideways was vital to success. Lominger's research, as summarized here, confirmed our impressions:

> At their best, peer relationships provide emotional support, spur professional growth, impart cultural and political knowledge, encourage collaboration and innovation, and extend personal influence.
>
> That's why the best organizations don't leave this to chance. They understand that productive peer relationships increase engagement and drive organizational performance. So they actively promote networking, collaboration, and communities of practice. Good things happen in those firms as peers develop personal relationships and trust in each other. Those relationships reduce friction in the organization. The gears of organizational change get lubricated. Work gets done faster. People look out for each other. Mistakes decrease. Quality and customer service improves. Information is shared more freely. Feedback is provided more freely and candidly. Resources are used more efficiently. Business becomes fun, engaging.[a]

a. M. M. Lombardo and R. E. Eichinger, *FYI: For Your Improvement,* 5th ed. (Minneapolis: Lominger International, a Korn/Ferry Company, 2009).

As we mentioned in chapter 3, a key aspect of this involvement comes in the form of improved information flow and use. Whether it is information on what changes are affecting a business partner's market, on the struggles a peer is having with his or her own team, or on the personal pressures a colleague is having, the open and inclusive style of the high-performing CIOs enables them to have more and better information earlier. This allows them to respond more effectively, not only because

WHO IS YOUR PRIMARY TEAM?

"In a management exercise with my vice presidents, I asked them to talk about their team," Steve Stone, Lowe's CIO, recalls. "They all immediately began discussing their functional area of responsibility and the people who worked for them.

"After everyone had spoken, I said, 'The people in this room—your colleagues—are your team, not the folks that report to you. There, you are a coach. Here in this room, you are a team member. You are part of a team of coaches for the organization, and it is critical for this team to be cohesive and aligned for the overall IT organization to deliver results.'

"It's no different for me. My team is the people at the CXO level. That means the horizontal relationships with my peers are vital."

they have more time, but also because they are getting the information in context from a trusted peer, someone who will be allied with them in going forward (as in the case of Runcie and the school principal).

The other incredible point about managing sideways is that it actually aids in your upward relationships. As your peers become your trusted and respected allies, their impact on the CEO's perception of you works in your favor.

And speaking of the relationship with the CEO, that is where we turn our attention next.

THE CIO-CEO RELATIONSHIP

Let's be blunt: far too few CEOs view their CIOs as true business leaders and peers to other members of their executive team. And yet as we stated in the introduction, this is increasingly what CEOs expect (and need), given the pervasive and pivotal contribution that IT makes to business performance across the twenty-first-century enterprise.

By contrast, one of the key things we observed in high-performing CIOs was the strength and quality of their relationships with their CEOs and boards of directors. We heard example after example of CIOs who had forged deep and collaborative CEO relationships; earned a level of trust to the point that CEOs often seek their private advice and counsel regarding cross-enterprise opportunities and other issues (in part due to their unique view of the entire organization from the CIO seat); enjoyed access to the CEO way beyond formal meetings and decisions processes; and, in short, became a confidant to their CEO.

So what's different about these CIOs? Well, it starts with their ability to deliver—they pay particular attention to the need for IT to come through on time and on budget for their peers. In other words, they act just like any other *business* leader in the organization. Then, they actively manage any uniqueness in the CEO relationship. But, most important, they enjoy success with the CEO and board because at the foundation of all their interactions are the same people-leadership skills we've spoken about throughout this book. We will expand on this shortly. But first, note that these observations were further reinforced by the research from our Gartner Executive Programs colleagues Colleen Young and Dave Aron, who found that only 15 percent of CIO-CEO relationships could be described as a "trusted-ally" relationship (figure 4-1).[6]

Let's dig a little deeper and see how the best CIOs find themselves in the upper right quadrant of the figure. The first noted characteristic of high performers, as we just mentioned, is delivery of results. Delivering results provides the initial credibility from which to cultivate the CEO relationship, but actually starts with horizontal relationships. As Young and Aron noted, "a close relationship with the CEO is built upon a partnering relationship with business unit leaders. That relationship, in turn, is built upon transactional excellence against business unit

FIGURE 4-1

CIO influence directly correlates to relationship value with CEO

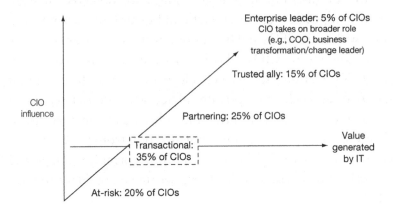

Source: Colleen Young and Dave Aron, "Identifying CEO Expectations and Delivering Against Them," Gartner Executive Programs Report, August 2009.

demand streams. CIOs who have achieved a trusted-ally relationship with the CEO are credited with consistently delivering against business unit leader expectations. They tie their success to business unit leader success and proactively manage business unit leader relationships, spending exponentially more individual time with leadership peers than with the CEO or even their own IT team."

Second, high-performing CIOs understand they have to overcome certain natural barriers to a true CEO-CIO alliance as you will see later in figure 4-2. Not all CEOs are created equal,

Managing business unit relationships and delivering against business unit leader priorities are, in many ways, more important than delivering against the priorities of the CEO.
A relationship of trust and credibility with the CEO is an outcome of delivering against immediate business unit needs, not a prerequisite.

and high-performing CIOs spend the time understanding their CEO's drivers and personality, and respond in kind. These CIOs also understand that there are certain natural resistance factors to relationships from the CEO's point of view, and they actively manage these natural barriers (table 4-1).

The last characteristic, but one that enables all others, is the high performer's commitment to people skills. As we interviewed high performers, we consistently saw that they had the ability to forge the right relationships. That is, underlying their

TABLE 4-1

Overcoming natural barriers to a true CEO-CIO alliance

CEO resistance factors	Remediation tactics
CEOs primarily invest in relationships that facilitate realization of enterprise goals.	• Put all conversations, including those tracked in executive compensation plans, in the context of specific business goals and objectives. • Provide insight and advice regarding enterprisewide opportunities for performance improvement and key risk-management factors of interest at CEO and board level.
CEOs are disinclined to involve themselves in operations.	• Ensure IT operations excellence, hence, making this a nonissue at CEO level. • Keep conversations strategic and always business focused at level appropriate to CEO.
CEOs are insecure about their understanding of IT.	• Be a trusted source of education and IT literacy—always contextualized to your CEO's situation and key business issues at hand. • Educate in a way that matches your CEO's style and ensures he or she can ask questions and be involved without losing face—often one on one.
CEOs want to add value to the IT conversation.	• Communicate, share ideas, and seek counsel early, rather than requiring intervention later on issues needing CEO direction. • Ensure that key decisions are made in a well-informed and timely manner.

Source: Adapted from Colleen Young and Dave Aron, "Identifying CEO Expectations and Delivering Against Them," Gartner Executive Programs Report, August 2009.

understanding of the uniqueness of the CEO relationship and their sensitivity to the impact of horizontal relationships on upward relationships is their obvious commitment to people leadership. It bears repeating that each of these CIOs first committed to being open, being approachable, mastering communications, and the like, and then leveraged those competencies in creating the type of trusted relationship they enjoy with peers, CEO, and the board. And, it's right in line with what we saw in figure 4-1. As the CIO role evolves, and the dependency on IT as an enabling tool to win in the marketplace rises, so do the enterprise's expectations for the IT organization and the CIO relationship—hence, the critical dependence on superior people skills.

Dick Gochnauer, CEO of United Stationers, and his CIO, Dave Bent, are a prime example. United Stationers is a company that has evolved over the last decade from a traditional wholesale distributor to one that understands that "information" enables modern logistics success and that value-added services are a critical aspect of customer relationships, revenue, and profitability moving forward. Gochnauer describes his relationship with his CIO:

> I view my relationship with Dave in a similar way as anyone else on my direct report team—that of a peer business leader. I expect him to be a thought leader not only regarding technology-related matters, but also on early visibility, advice and counsel regarding enterprisewide opportunities, and issues from a broader business perspective. I value the insight that Dave (and key members of his IT team) have by virtue of their IT role, for example, their ability to spot early indicators that a business program may be going off track, or identify strategic opportunities on how we can better engage customers and consumers using online techniques.[7]

As Bent describes the frequency and type of interactions, the level of the CEO-CIO relationship and mutual trust becomes clear: "When we are both in the office, it is not uncommon for us to meet just about every day." This could be as part of formal decision-making meetings (i.e., quarterly IT portfolio meetings that Bent chairs, board technology committee half-day meetings five times a year, CEO staff meetings every two weeks that frequently contain IT-enabled business-change agenda items), and more ad hoc meetings based on emerging strategic ideas (including regular white-board sessions) or troubleshooting issues that may arise.

When asked about the secret to the relationship success, Bent is quick to point out that his "biggest focus is on open dialog and trust." He explains that if he is to be viewed as a trusted adviser at this level, he has to be able to have candid conversations. Beyond that, Bent ensures that conversations are always focused on the business issue at hand and tailored to Gochnauer's personality type and decision-making style. For example, "I know Dick hates to be surprised by bad news and therefore values early involvement and collaboration around key initiatives or major issues."[8] So while Bent admits he has suffered from the inevitable bumps in the road during his tenure as CIO, having the right CEO relationship—along with those with his business peers—has enabled him personally and the IT organization to maximize their contributions to business results. In a further sign of the payoff, Bent was recently promoted. In addition to his role as CIO, he now also has profit-and-loss responsibility for a new e-business services unit.

This approach works, and it works well. When you deliver, manage the uniqueness of relationships, and engage superb people-leadership skills, great things happen. "We just came through a strategic planning process where we went into amazing detail about what the university is going to spend over the next two years," American University's Swartz told us in late spring of 2009. "I had spent the previous year, my first at the university, delivering on every aspect of our plan and turning around all of our relationships with my peers. And even though we were in the most difficult economic times in thirty years, I got about a double-digit budget increase over the significant increase

I got last year. On top of that, the CFO suggested that we figure out how to make other departments add as much value and work as well as IT does."

RELATIONSHIPS 101

We've discussed horizontal, or peer, relationships and CIO-to-CEO relationships. Additionally, we've touched on the relationships you need to form with those outside the organization (vendors, system integrators, joint ventures, and business partnerships across the supply chain). But whether you are discussing those relationships or the ones we have not mentioned, we discovered that the highest performers focus on the same core ingredients for success no matter whom they are interacting with:

1. *They first create a foundation of trust.* They do what they say they are going to do, whether it is delivering on workplace commitments or acting in a consistent and honorable manner—particularly when the going gets tough.

2. *They establish an environment of mutual respect.* No deep relationship can exist without it. This begins with the top performers' ability to perform their job extremely well. (So trust, in large part, is a result of integrity plus competency. No one respects someone who either can't do the work or can't do it well.) And then they know both how to give and how to hold ground. They are not just order takers. They know how to say no. This is important (and takes us full circle on this point) because winning is collaborative and requires mutual respect in order to get the best work done.

3. *They create a personal connection where the parties can relate to each other's situation.* Top performers

push themselves to learn multiple personal and professional motivators about each person, so that they have an opportunity to find connections. Then, having created the foundation of personal understanding, both they and the person they are dealing with are able to weather difficult times or major conflicts with greater ease (another example of soft skills' yielding hard results).

4. *They work on the relationships constantly.* They understand that relationships can wither and die, so they actively nurture and manage them. At the same time, these top CIOs know that not all relationships are equal, and so these leaders actively carve out the time to cultivate the most important ones.

To establish this trust and foster winning relationships, high-performing CIOs draw heavily on the core interpersonal competencies described in chapter 3. The CIOs show that they care and are open and receptive, two attributes that make it substantially easier for a relationship to form. And they use these relationships, often outside formal channels, to collaborate on and influence future key decisions.

The point here is that most CIOs underestimate both the time it takes to deliver a winning relationship and the power and payback it can create later on. Nevertheless, the highest-performing CIOs are hyperfocused on forging the right relationships as the primary means to drive business results.

When trusted, respected relationships are in place, they are a catalyst for highly effective, collaborative decision making. Conversely, when the winning ingredients of relationships do not exist or are fragile at best, even the simplest set of decisions can go dramatically south, hurting the effectiveness of IT and the broader business results.

Relationships are enhanced via the core interpersonal competencies such as caring, relating, and being open and receptive. With the relationship in place, each party can work productively through tough trade-offs and find a mutually agreeable solution to which they can both commit.

"If I have deep relationships in place," says Marv Adams, former president and CIO of Fidelity Shared Services, "my colleagues across the business don't hesitate in terms of trusting me when issues get really substantial in their area. That makes it easier for us to work together to try to figure out what to do about those issues."[9]

This, as Tom Tabor, CIO of Highmark, points out, is something you need to constantly work at. Tabor, for example, questions each of his team members on knowing the professional, financial, and personal goals of their peers. "If I don't understand—if my team members don't understand—what motivates a peer to action, then the relationship is unpredictable. I want my team to develop relationships to the point that they can tell me how their peers are motivated from a career perspective, from a company perspective, and from a personal perspective. It's only then that you can begin to truly understand the person on the other side of the relationship and know how to approach them."[10]

WATCH YOUR STEP: NAVIGATING POLITICAL LAND MINES

As we build relationships in every direction, the inevitable will occur: "The CIO will encounter a predictable set of political land mines that have nothing to do with the technical merits of the decision at hand," our Gartner colleague Tina Nunno writes in her research paper, "CIO Political Land Mines and How to Avoid Them."

More specifically, she argues that there are four predictable land mines you are bound to encounter. The very nature of the

---

Politics and business outcomes are closely related. CIOs who
have good strategies and great ideas but cannot influence
key stakeholders will find it difficult to succeed.

CIO role guarantees it. The turf wars will be over these politically charged issues:

- *Resource scarcity.* The amount of money, people,
  and projects that can be initiated is limited, and
  every department wants more than its fair share.
  When resources are scarce and the organization has
  not spent a lot of time thinking about how to handle
  the inevitable conflicts, this land mine is easily triggered.

- *Control.* Who decides how things will be done? Who
  creates the timelines and decides on the deliverables?
  Many IT-related capabilities and initiatives affect
  the way enterprises do their day-to-day work. When
  technology-initiated changes are perceived as an IT
  power-grab, turf wars can result. For many managers,
  no battle is too small when control is at stake.

- *Status.* As CIOs increasingly work on enterprisewide
  initiatives, different stakeholders will have different
  requirements, not all of which are possible to fulfill.
  Inevitably, some players feel they will win and some
  feel they will lose, and where losing means loss of face,
  the status land mine can be particularly forceful.

- *Core beliefs.* It can be extremely difficult to get an
  organization to alter the foundation on which it was
  based. Individuals, groups, and enterprises often have
  strong beliefs about what makes them successful,
  where their strengths lie, and what does or doesn't
  work for them. IT provides data and information that

can threaten core organizational beliefs. When it does, the affected people and departments can lash out.

As we said, these land mines are inevitable. Being the victim of one is not.

The strength of a CIO's relationships, particularly the horizontal relationships with peers discussed earlier in this chapter, is a central factor in tripping, defusing, or avoiding political land mines. The high-performing CIOs we interviewed were incredibly aware of political dynamics. They told us that when they face one of the political land mines we just discussed they draw on their social-participative leadership style to forge authentic, trusted (and, in many cases, more personal) relationships to defuse the situation.

In wrapping up this section on politics, we must stress the overriding imperative: *avoid integrity traps.* Relationships at their core are built on a foundation of trust. Trust that takes immense effort and time to earn, however, can be destroyed in the briefest of moments. The highest-performing CIOs treasure this trust above all else—never compromising their integrity for a short-term gain. They focus their energy on creating authentic and enduring relationships, assets that enable them to navigate the challenging and dangerous terrain of the CIO role and that reduce the risks associated with tripping the inevitable land mines.

Whether your relationships are keeping you safe by allowing you to avoid political land mines or are helping you collaboratively drive business results, the payoff from the right relationships is huge (figure 4-2).

Drawing on both your social-participative leadership style and the relationships you have created is the best way to successfully combat the internal politics you are bound to encounter.

FIGURE 4-2

Forging the right relationships maximizes your reach, enabling collaborative delivery of results

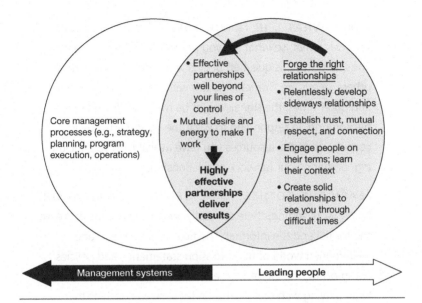

Core management processes (e.g., strategy, planning, program execution, operations)

• Effective partnerships well beyond your lines of control
• Mutual desire and energy to make IT work

Highly effective partnerships deliver results

Forge the right relationships

• Relentlessly develop sideways relationships
• Establish trust, mutual respect, and connection
• Engage people on their terms; learn their context
• Create solid relationships to see you through difficult times

Management systems

Leading people

CALL TO ACTION

If you haven't yet established the right relationships with the right people, consider the following tips for development:

CREATE A RELATIONSHIP INVESTMENT STRATEGY. Relationships take time to build, and time is a finite resource, so choose wisely. Determine which relationships are going to be the most critical to you—don't overlook those critical sideways relationships. The relationships that matter now might not be the same ones that will make a difference three to five years down the road, and vice versa. Also, evaluate the current strength of those relationships, and allocate your time in relationship building accordingly. Finally, don't shy away from the relationships that are the most difficult to develop, but are most critical to your success.

ASK, "WHAT'S IN IT FOR THEM?" Relationships are a two-way street, so what are you providing to the other party? The answer to this question begins with understanding what others' needs are. Sometimes, this will come right out at you, and other times, the signals might be more subtle and in the background. In responding to what the other party needs, consider all of the resources you have available to you, including, perhaps, your network of relationships.

LEARN THE "OTHER" SIDE OF THE ORGANIZATION. In any work setting, there are really two organizations that exist, the formal and the informal. The first is often a clear and well-defined world of titles, mission statements, and policies and procedures. The other is a more ambiguous, sometimes logic-defying web of unwritten rules and relationships that don't fit cleanly on an organizational chart. Success requires understanding both. To learn the latter, look and listen closer; not everything is what it appears to be on the surface.

MAKE YOUR MOVE. Don't wait for relationships to find you. Take the initiative, and work to actively shape others' perceptions. This may be a challenge for the naturally introverted among us, but consider the alternative. No one succeeded (at least not for very long) by taking a passive approach to relationship building.

NAVIGATE POLITICS WITH INTEGRITY. You face some unique political land mines, by the very nature of your CIO role. Don't let your fear of politics and the ambiguity that accompanies it lead you to avoid politically charged situations or neglect developing your political skills. Instead, hunker down and draw on the social-participative leadership style and the interpersonal skills that improve information flow and your listening to proactively predict and defuse these land mines. In doing so, remember to treasure your integrity at all times.

SUMMING UP

Winning relationships are built on a foundation of trust and authenticity, things that are enhanced by the CIO's social-participative style. Because the best CIOs relate well, care about people, and are open and receptive, they are able to create stronger and deeper relationships.

Why are winning relationships important? Three reasons. First is the one we have talked about throughout. As the number and complexity of interactions we have with people explode—that is, as it becomes more and more important to get the work done through others (and the others increasingly do not report to us)—having good relationships will make it far easier to get things done. (And good relationships dramatically increase the chances that things will be done well and will have more impact.) Second, people work harder, better, and more effectively when they are working with people whom they truly like, trust, and respect. Third, when the invariable bumps in the road occur and a project starts to get off track, it is far easier to get things going again in the right direction when there is a solid relationship in place among the people who need to get the work done.

All this explains why you need to develop relationships. (Keep in mind that establishing relationships doesn't end at the walls of your building. They need to extend to all key stakeholders. That means, of course, that you need to adapt for global and cultural differences.)

The next question is, What relationships do you need to develop? The answer is that you must manage up, down, *and* particularly sideways. As we have seen, the sideways relationships are often the most critical to getting our jobs done. Paradoxically, as we have discovered in doing our research, peer relationships are those that many CIOs spend the least amount of time on.

The takeaway from this chapter is clear: the bar is being raised. You will need to master a greater quantity—and breadth—of relationships. You will need to invest time, attention, and passion to create true relationships that can help you deliver on the promise of IT.

Why? Ultimately, it is the power of the right relationships that allows you to produce the right results.

MASTER COMMUNICATIONS: ALWAYS AND ALL WAYS

COMPELLING THE ACTION YOU NEED

Owen McCall, CIO of the Warehouse Group, was trying to think of a way of communicating a pivotal part of leadership. As he remembered a recent vacation, he hit on a powerful metaphor:

> We were on holiday and went to Franz Josef Glacier in New Zealand. As you walk along the glacier, there is a river lined with rocks the perfect height for jumping off, if you are a five-year-old boy.
>
> My son, Ryan, would climb on a rock that was maybe a foot high, jump off into the nearest clear space, climb up a different rock, and jump off again, because that is what five-year-old boys do.
>
> Well, it was growing late and the rest of the family had gone on ahead to get ready for dinner. I hung back

with Ryan, and he kept climbing up and jumping off rocks.

Eventually I said, "Look, Ryan, you need to stop because we need to catch up with everyone." So I took his hand and started walking toward the rest of the group. And as five-year-old boys do, he got very tired very quickly once he was not doing what he wanted. After about a dozen steps, he said, "Dad, carry me, carry me."

Well, we had a ways to go to the lodge, and five-year-olds can be a handful to carry. That's when I realized that what I needed to do was not stop him from jumping on rocks, but get him to jump on the rocks along the path back to the lodge.

I said, "Ryan, see how many rocks you can jump on between here and that next tree" (which was down the path toward the lodge). So he ran down the path, jumping on rocks, then jumping off, and then running to the next one. When I caught up to him at the tree, I said, "See if you can beat your own record by the time we get to the next one." He ran off again, and we continued doing this until we got to the lodge. He had a tremendous amount of fun, and we got there in time.

I thought about this later and realized that as leaders, too often we kill people's passions by saying the equivalent of "Stop jumping off those rocks. You need to go this way and do this."

A better approach is to guide people's passions. Don't stop them from climbing and jumping off rocks, but get them to climb and jump off rocks in the right direction.

Let's stop killing people's passions and harness those passions instead.[1]

IT IS A WONDERFUL story, and it clearly captures one of the key traits the best CIOs use in communicating. They get their

> Why is communication so important? If you can't articulate
> your vision and ideas and convince people to follow,
> then you can't lead.

points across in a way that is personal, authentic, and relatable and clarifies what action they want people to take. ("Let's stop killing people's passions and harness those passions instead.")

But they do more than that. The best CIOs are aware they are always communicating, with the tone of their voice, their word selection, their body language, their energy level, and, oh yes, what they actually say. Because they know they are always sending a message, they make sure they are communicating effectively in *all* ways—up, down, and sideways.

Finally, high-performing CIOs are constantly *listening*, not only to make sure that their message is being received but also to see if they are hearing and learning things that can help refine what they have to say. In so doing, the CIOs can make an even closer connection to their audience—be it one person or the entire organization.

Let's walk through all this, starting with something that you may not have thought a lot about.

1. ALWAYS COMMUNICATING

What does the way you communicate tell others about you as a leader? Everything.

> Perception is reality. The perception of the IT organization's
> credibility, role in the enterprise, and value, and the perception of
> you as a leader, are shaped by all your communications to everyone
> both inside and outside your enterprise.

And people's perception is reality. If you cannot effectively influence perceptions, then you leave them to chance, putting yourself at a huge disadvantage.

Richard Gius describes the way he thinks of all this in terms of the "shadow of the leader": "What I know now, that was difficult for me to understand early in my career, is the image that you project as a leader has a huge impact on the morale of your team and the support you receive from your business partners. The image I project and the confidence, or the urgency, or the passion I put forth are things that I have worked really hard on during the course of my career."[2]

This was a consistent theme when we talked with the best CIOs. At some point in their career, they came to realize that they were always communicating—whether they meant to be or not.

Gerald Shields of Aflac tells a wonderful story that makes the point:

> I was distracted—I was dealing with a bunch of problems simultaneously—when three of my people came to see me about a problem *they* had been working on. They said they had found a solution.
>
> I asked them to explain it to me, and when they were done—and again, I wasn't giving them my full attention—I said, "If that's what you think is best, it's fine with me." And with that, I went back to doing what I was doing.
>
> A couple of days later, I saw them all together in a meeting room, so I popped my head in and asked them what they were doing. And they told me they were working on a solution to the problem I thought they had solved.
>
> "Two days ago, you told me you had a good solution."
>
> They said, "Yeah, but we could tell you didn't like it."
>
> I said, "I thought it was a good solution. I told you that."

They said, "Nope. We could tell by your body language and your energy level and how you responded to it, you didn't like it."

I said, "No, you told me that was the best solution. That's good; I'm cool with it."

"That's not what we heard."

"But that's what I said."

They told me, "That's what you said with your words; that's not what you said with the way you answered us."

They hadn't believed me, even though I meant it.

It flatters as much as it angers me, but the fact is, every twitch I have occurs under a spotlight. I can't ignore it. This is the hardest part of the job for me, understanding how I impact the organization with my energy level, my wording, my enthusiasm, and how I treat people.[3]

While they may not like it, executives such as Shields and Gius understand that they must master "always" communications, the fact that they are constantly (i.e., always) sending a message, whether they mean to or not.

Because high-performing CIOs know they are always communicating, they consistently monitor to see if they, and the people on the other end, are in sync. The CIOs are also constantly checking how others perceive them so that they can reinforce the desired values, behaviors, and actions. Not surprisingly, because

---

A POTENTIALLY TROUBLING QUESTION

Imagine that a documentary-style camera followed you around all day and recorded your interactions with everyone at work. If you sat down at the end of the day and watched the playback, would you like what you saw? What would your communications convey (or not convey) to others about your leadership?

---

they take this approach, all their communications—from the seemingly casual comment to a major presentation—are more effective. There is also another advantage in taking this approach. By spending so much time thinking about and planning your core messages, you can be more effective in your daily and unplanned (i.e., a quick conversation in the hall) communications, because you know exactly what you need to get across. All this naturally leads to the next point.

2. COMMUNICATING ALL WAYS

The good CIOs understand the power of communications. The great ones build a discipline around it. They go about it the way an excellent project manager handles an assignment: they think through requirements; they understand their audiences; they plot out success factors and potential risks; and they know what needs to be delivered and when. And when they do deliver, they seek feedback and make the necessary adjustments to produce the desired results.

They continually strive to execute effectively, whether they are making a formal presentation or having a casual encounter in the halls. While their conversation with someone at the water cooler can appear to be extemporaneous, the reality is the underlying core messages have been well thought out. Breaking it down, the core messages of high-performing CIOs tend to have four characteristics in common. The best CIOs tell us that when it comes to communication, you need to make sure that you are: (1) purpose-driven in your approach; (2) consistent, constant,

---

The high performers make it a discipline to think through communications needs—in the process, they plan for the unplanned encounter.

---

and in context; (3) personal and authentic; and (4) easy to relate to. Because our research has shown that so many less-than-great CIOs failed in at least one of these areas, let's briefly run through them one at a time.

Purpose-Driven

Saying your communication needs to be purpose-driven is accurate, but a bit abstract. So let's try to bring it down from the high-altitude level and see what it means in day-to-day terms.

When we say all your communication needs to be purpose-driven, what we are really saying is that before every interaction, you want to ask yourself this question: What am I trying to accomplish?

If you do, you will end up with the same conclusion every time: I want the person (or people) I am communicating with to do X. The X could be a specific thing, like "deliver outstanding project results going beyond just being on time and on budget," or the understanding of a critical part of their job, such as "we are the department that has to make every other part of the organization work to its maximum potential."

Understanding that the most powerful communications are ones that motivate an individual to take a specific action, Richard Gius says, "I try to make sure the larger vision always translates into what I call hundreds and hundreds of micro-visions, the way my team sees how they do their jobs. If I say my vision is to transform IT into a world-class organization, or best-in-class in our industry, that doesn't mean a lot to my network engineer or my help-desk person. But if I say that's our vision and then communicate in a meaningful way to individual teams, say, for example, my project management group, here's what we need to do to make that vision a reality—we need to be on time and on budget—then they understand it and what it means for them."

Sherry Aaholm of FedEx agrees and underscores the effort that you have to commit to do this: "Early in my career, I dealt

POP QUIZ

Think back on a recent plan or other issue about which you communicated. Take an informal survey of people in all directions—up,
down, and sideways. Test to see how consistently they answer questions about what you intended to communicate.

a lot with a lot of customers, and so I got to understand the
sales mentality. And that is what you are really doing here. You
are selling your ideas and your vision, and that means you need
to connect to something that resonates with your audience."[4]

Here's an example of how this plays out in practice from a
CIO who asked not to be identified:

> Each quarter, in an effort to develop IT literacy across
> the organization, I choose a new technology, an IT
> gadget, or an IT trend (once it was the signal boost
> packs you can add to your mobile phone; most recently,
> it was social networking sites). I look at the topic, I study
> the press, I speak with my architects and my CTO [chief
> technology officer], and then I sit and think. I treat it as
> a PR issue. What are my main messages, and to which
> audiences? Then, after all that work, I *never* actually
> make any formal presentation. Why? Because presenta-
> tions bore people—and sometimes, I swear they think
> I am trying to sell them a used car.
>
> Rather, I focus that quarter on using the opportunities,
> such as lunch in the cafeteria; waiting at the elevator; or
> using the time before a meeting starts, when 80 percent
> are waiting for the last 20 percent to show up—any
> opportunity I can—to work what I have learned into
> the conversation.

But what is surprising to them, and effective, I hope, is that I can speak clearly, concisely, and in terms that this particular business audience would care about—because I have thought it all out in advance. Hey, I may not come off as nonchalant as I think I do, but I can tell you this: over the past year, I can definitely feel an improvement in the quality of technology-related questions I get from the business. Something's working.

Clearly, getting your intent across is necessary, but not sufficient for effective communication. A certain amount of finesse is needed to take communication to the next level. It begins with the art of messaging.

Consistent, Constant, and in Context

Can you change the way you word your message? Absolutely, and you should. People process information in different ways. And they get bored hearing the same idea expressed the same way time after time.

Can you change the way you present the message? Yes, again.

But can the substance of your message—the things you believe and stand for—change? Absolutely not.

You always want people to know what is important, where you stand, and where they should concentrate their attention. That way, there is no wasted effort and everyone is pulling in the same direction. When they are, it is an extremely powerful force, as Filippo Passerini, P&G's CIO, points out: "We constantly survey our employees at all levels around the world, and our research shows that the majority of our people are able to give you a good elevator conversation on what we stand for and what we want to focus on."[5] By continually repeating the importance of customer focus in speeches to large groups, small groups, and in one-on-one sessions, Passerini has gotten the message to resonate.

As you see, this doesn't happen by accident. You need to constantly communicate the points you want to get across. As successful CIO after successful CIO told us, it is impossible to deliver the same message too many times.

This can be a difficult idea for many managers—especially those who came up on the technical side of the organization—to comprehend. They don't understand why repetition is necessary. They think if they say it once, it should be enough. Well, it isn't.

As nice as it would be to believe, people are simply not hanging on to your every word or committing your e-mails and memos to memory. Their lack of attention is not malicious. It is just that they are distracted. There is that project that was due yesterday, the fire that needs to be put out now, and the unhappy colleague who has just sent off her third e-mail in twenty-three minutes, demanding that something be done to help her now! That's why you want to deliver the same message (using different words and different techniques) over and over again.

Ramón Baez, CIO of Kimberly-Clark, told us how he came to embrace this position: "I read the bios of many of the great leaders in history like Mahatma Gandhi, Winston Churchill, Martin Luther King, and the like. What I found to be an incredible common characteristic is their ability to repeat, via simple methods, over and over and over again. In Mahatma Gandhi's case, for example, he must have spoken thousands of hours in his life to different multitudes of people, and he always appeared to have the same three or four messages. I think about that as I plan my own communications."[6]

Constantly delivering clear and consistent messages helps create an "organizational memory" around what is important, what people need to do, and what success looks like.

As Gius puts it, "You just have to overcommunicate, overcommunicate, overcommunicate. The more I communicate, the better the results seem to be. And what I also notice is the less I communicate, or the more I assume people got the message, the more I'm surprised that they didn't—and how underwhelming the results are."

Personal and Authentic

Organizational charts can be misleading. Sure, they lay out a formal reporting structure, but as everyone knows, you can't pick names at random, put them in one of the boxes on the chart, and expect the same results. People are not inspired to do their best work because they are led by some rectangle on the org chart. They are led by Bill Smith, CIO, or Sally Jones, head of software development. And they are simply more likely to pay attention to, and go the extra mile for, someone they see as a real person, as opposed to an executive they see as just another empty suit. (In this regard, they are absolutely no different from you.) This is why you want to be seen as a real person, someone who is open and receptive, caring, and authentic, as we discussed in chapter 3.

Authenticity is just as important when it comes to dealing with stakeholders outside your company's walls—joint ventures partners and the like. You need to influence and persuade them, since they don't work for you directly, and you have a better chance of doing that if you are seen as a real person, someone they can relate to and respect.

This last observation is no small point. You need to be respected and seen as authentic and consistent because the cliché "Actions speak louder than words" is absolutely correct. You need to model the behavior you want. If you talk about teamwork, but hog the spotlight, or if you write e-mails about the importance of innovation, yet publicly punish well-intentioned mistakes, then people will find out very quickly and will either stop paying attention to your message or, even worse, dismiss your message altogether.

Yes, you want your communication to be authentic and personal, but equally important, you want to make sure it is embraced. That means you need to create a connection with your audience. What does your message mean to the recipient? How do I want him or her to act differently? If the connection doesn't occur, the communication hasn't occurred.

But—and it is a big *but*—communication is not just about tying what you have to say with what you want to accomplish; it is critical that the communication also be directly related to your audience's situation. People need to understand not only what you are saying, but also how it affects them.

There is no doubt that Owen McCall's story about his son came across as authentic and personal. It was clearly tied to his own situation. Everyone in the audience could picture McCall—"Dad" to Ryan—trying to cope with an extremely energetic son. But by the end of the speech, it was also clear what McCall wanted his listeners to do after they heard the anecdote. He was exhorting people to spend some time thinking about how to channel the enthusiasm of their employees, instead of thwarting it.

Relatable

A cornerstone of all communications is the need to tailor your message to your target audience. Especially in the technology world, where your business partners' literacy varies dramatically, the need to communicate at their level is critical. The highest performers communicate so that others can relate and, therefore, motivate the desired action.

Indeed, our research indicates that they are masters at the use of stories and metaphors. For example, McCall's audience "got it" because he opened his speech with something that was universal. Even the people in the audience who didn't have kids recognized what he was talking about, in describing his son's behavior. McCall triggered that response by tailoring his story for managers concerned about getting the best out of their employees.

When we asked CIOs how they developed their ability to use metaphors, many people spoke about how they learned first to respect the role of communication early in their lives. As Ross Philo of the U.S. Postal Service put it, "I can't say that today I consciously sit and think of what metaphor to use in each situation. It comes a bit naturally. But I think that's because I recognized early on how critical it was to connect my idea to someone else's understanding. So, I was always aware of metaphors, and I tucked them away. I read a lot, I write a lot, and those activities make me aware of useful metaphors. As a result, I have a whole portfolio of metaphors in my head that I can now call on in different situations."[7]

Another means of connecting is by focusing on what needs to happen—putting each person in the mode of thinking about what the goal is. President and CEO of Northwestern Memorial Hospital Dean Harrison explained the communication style of his CIO, Tim Zoph: "Tim's strength is being able to simply state a project goal and the most efficient and effective way to accomplish it; whether we are talking about installing a new system or improving or changing a system. He does not try and explain the intricacies of the technology."[8]

Sandra Camelo dos Santos, CIO of São Francisco's hydro-electric company in Brazil, says, "We work hard with our

---

The acid test is not whether you feel good about the communication. Rather it is this: Did people internalize your message? Did they move from awareness to understanding, to buy-in, and ultimately to commitment to action?

---

communication department each year to help us craft communications campaigns to make sure that IT's values, goals, and contributions are understood—and supported. In fact, we recently took advantage of the fact that we are in a heavy agricultural area and used the agriculture metaphor of planting and harvesting to gain buy-in to our latest campaign on process and how following process now yields great results down the road. I can't make them understand me; I have to make me understandable to them."[9]

How do you know when you are truly connecting? One CEO gave us his own litmus test: "When the audience walks away, I don't want them to just understand *what* I said; I want them to *feel* it."

3. LISTENING

Asked to define the three most critical competencies needed by CIOs today, Camelo dos Santos hit immediately on the importance of listening: "We are bombarded with information, and we in turn bombard others with information. It is crucial to be attentive and know how to listen in order to decode messages received. I also have to be able to decode external messages, on behalf of my team, so they can relate and be more tightly integrated to the rest of the business."

Most people think of communication as a two-way exchange of thoughts, feelings, or ideas. To take this a bit further, the ultimate success of communications is the extent to which a message is received and embraced toward a shared outcome.

Core to the central notion of communications as a two-way process is the ability to listen and to seek, accept, and act on feedback. But this simple definition of successful communication, however, is all too often overlooked in the clutter of everything else that is going on.

Listening is the ultimate way of demonstrating that it is not all about you and your agenda, and listening is also an excellent tool for breaking down barriers and getting more out of what you do with others. Indeed, the Lominger research indicates that the ability to listen is a "saving grace," a quality or redeeming feature that makes up for other generally negative characteristics. Unfortunately, the research also indicates that few executives are good listeners. How sad that something with so much potential is so poorly executed.

To ensure that you do indeed listen well, you might want to revisit the basics. Make sure you aren't sending any unplanned messages by furrowing your brow or fidgeting. Also, great listeners ask lots of questions. Finally, challenge yourself to ask someone you trust what you do when you are not listening, and set to work on eliminating those conversation enders. Feedback is also a form of listening.

Remember that old Zen-like riddle "If a tree falls in the forest and no one sees or hears it fall, did it really happen?" Well, on one level, of course it did. The tree fell. That is the premise of the riddle. But the question is a good one because it goes to what information was received. No one saw or heard the tree fall, so you can legitimately wonder if it fell.

It's the same with your message. If you say something, send out an e-mail, or give a speech and no one pays attention, then it is as if you haven't communicated at all.

But just having your audience receive a message is not enough. You need to create some sort of feedback system to see if the message was understood and that the recipients know what to do with the information.

In the hyperconnected world, communications are increasingly critical. If you can't see your message being received, how do you know it was? You listen for the feedback, through the feedback loop you established, as it works its way back to you.

For example, P&G's Passerini says his company does "a lot of formal and informal surveys with our business partners, and this feedback is part of the performance appraisal for our people. So there is a clear sense, in a very concrete, very material way, that it is important that we listen to our business partners. How well we do that is part of our reward system."

For most CIOs, the feedback loop is much more personal. It's making sure that they take the time to truly listen, to value and use the rich information from a two-way communication process to maximize their effectiveness as a leader. No matter how you do it, if you master communication, the payoff can be huge, as we see in figure 5-1.

FIGURE 5-1

Mastering communications enables a clarity and consistency of purpose that compels the right action

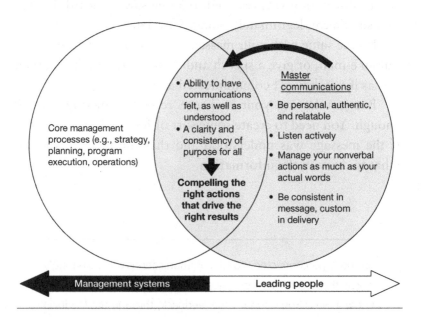

CALL TO ACTION

If things are still getting lost in translation between you and others, consider the following tips for development:

LISTEN WITH YOUR EYES (NOT JUST YOUR EARS).
Remember the last time you were in a situation where you were observing someone who was absolutely not connecting with his or her audience yet had no clue and just kept going right along? Painful, wasn't it? Avoid the same predicament, by watching your audience members carefully and reading their reactions, some of which may be subtle. Then make adjustments as you go and see if you are getting closer to the mark.

GET INSTANT PLAYBACK.   A good way to see if your message was received is to literally have others play it back to you in their own words. This is especially important if the message you are delivering is unique, complex, and important. The only trick with this approach is to make sure you don't deliver your request in a manner that comes across as condescending. Use a little self-deprecating humor if necessary, and underscore that you just wanted to make sure you were coming across as intended.

IT'S NOT JUST THE WORDS YOU ARE COMMUNICATING.
Just as others' nonverbal behavior conveys an important message about how you are being received, it also works the other way. One thing about nonverbal communication is that there are some things we do habitually (folding arms, clicking pens, staring out the window, etc.) that send a message we don't necessarily intend to send, yet we have no idea that this is the impact we are having.

ENLIST AN EXTRA PAIR OF EYES AND EARS. To the previous point, we all need to be much more aware of the impact we are really having. Enlist a colleague—someone you trust to give you honest feedback—as a communications watchdog. If you are in meetings or informal conversations together, have this person give you feedback (positive and negative) on how you came across and what adjustments you could make. It is especially helpful if this person has an awareness of some particular communication problem areas you are trying to address.

AX THE BUZZWORDS (AND THE TECHNICAL JARGON). Nothing undermines authenticity (and creates confusion) like an endless string of impressive-sounding words that add up to not much of anything. Don't hide behind your technical pedigree or your verbal gymnastics skills to connect with your audience. Just think about what you really want to convey, and then tweak that message by running it through the lens of your audience.

SUMMING UP

It is absolutely no accident that the highest-performing CIOs communicate so well—always, all ways. They know it is a pivotal part of their job, because if you cannot get across your ideas and persuade others to follow you, you cannot lead. That's why they place what can seem like a disproportionate emphasis on communicating in ways that their audience can relate to.

This doesn't occur by accident. The best CIOs work on their communication skills. They apply discipline to communication: thinking, planning, analyzing. They are constantly checking to make sure that the information they are trying to get across is clear, concise, and consistent. Equally important, they are always making sure that the points they are trying to make are not only being heard but are also understood and embraced. They are active listeners. They have learned to listen even when the message is something they don't want to hear. Through listening, they are not only learning new things, but also garnering the feedback they need to ensure that their messages are understood.

Why are these efforts important? The ultimate goal of any communication effort is to compel a desired action. Selling your ideas, inspiring and achieving results through others, building great relationships—all these activities hinge on great communications. That's why the best CIOs consider mastery of communication vitally important—all ways and always.

INSPIRE OTHERS

YOU CAN'T LEAD IF OTHERS WON'T FOLLOW

Marv Adams, former president of Fidelity Shared Services, which includes the technology, operations, and real estate divisions of the huge investment firm, was talking to us about the bosses he has had across his career, and he made a telling point.

> *I've been exposed to some really good leaders and some really bad ones across my career. With the good ones, I've seen the energy and alignment that gets created, how much you can get done, and how good people feel about their affiliation with the group. The best bosses inspire people who work for them to give it their all, as opposed to offering up the minimum. Invariably, it is that extra, discretionary effort that determines whether something succeeds.*
>
> *And with bad leaders, I've seen how quickly they can destroy trust, and how much stress gets created in the work environment, and just how negative an impact they can have on productivity. That's why it is so important to have a passion and enthusiasm to drive people to higher levels of performance.*[1]

THAT'S A POINT we heard repeatedly from the highest-performing CIOs. They talked—with passion and at great length—of the importance of getting people excited to accomplish great things via IT on behalf of the enterprise.

And what those CIOs say is a critical skill that is confirmed by Lominger's empirical research. The ability to inspire others is one of the three characteristics most highly correlated with executive success—the other two are the ability to create the new and different (which we will talk about later in the chapter) and the ability to make complex decisions (covered in chapter 2). Why is the ability to inspire so important? Because it is the best and most efficient way to move from vision to execution—it motivates people to obtain results. That's why the best CIOs devote an inordinate amount of time and energy to making sure they are inspiring others.

But while the research shows that inspiring others is vitally important, it also reveals something else: inspiring others is one of the least common competencies among leaders and managers today. Add to this the increasingly connected environment in which we are being asked to lead, one where more outcomes are outside our direct control, and we observe a trifecta of powerful forces converging to underline the pivotal role that your ability to inspire others plays in your success as CIO.

For these reasons, we as authors are particularly passionate about this topic, while simultaneously recognizing that it can be a great challenge. Indeed, in conducting research for, and writing, this book, it was this chapter that we struggled and agonized over the most. Inspiring others, and explaining how to inspire, can be elusive. That makes it hard to lay out a clear path that leads to effective implementation. But after extensive interviewing and research, we believe we have discovered the key.

It all starts from the premise that you can't lead if others will not follow. And people cannot follow if they do not know where you are going. This means that you need to begin with a vision—a vision to which others can connect and relate. But a vision by itself is useless. Once you have it, you must make it a reality. You must inspire others to action by managing vision and purpose, motivating others, and building effective teams. Let's talk about how to do all three.

STARTING WITH A VISION

Listen as three of the very best CIOs talk about creating a vision of a better future, the starting point if you ever plan to accomplish anything of significance:

- "What a vision gives, both to the people you are responsible for and to your internal customers, is hope. And from there it becomes a rallying cry, the thing that gets people to shoulder their responsibilities and get their chins to rise up. Vision is the number-one leadership trait you can have" (Phil Pavitt, CIO for HMRC [Her Majesty's Revenue and Customs department]).[2]

- "If you have a clear, compelling vision, one that gets people excited, you can keep the team with you, even in the worst situations. They'll stick with you, if they truly believe in the vision" (Sherry Aaholm, executive vice president of IT at Federal Express).[3]

- "If you don't have a clear vision of where you're trying to take an organization, people are going to be confused about what you're trying to accomplish. Nothing drives me crazier than leaders who are mushy on vision" (Richard Gius).[4]

Picturing what the new and different is going to look like has always been a key competency for CIOs, as the quotes make clear. But once you have come up with your vision, you need to make it a reality. The only way this is going to happen is if you inspire people to believe in the vision, to want to make your dream come to life.

Having the most well-thought-out vision and strategy means
nothing if your followers are not energized and motivated
to carry it out.

It sounds simple when we put it that way; however, it is anything but. Inspiring people to take action is the most important thing a CIO can do, and not surprisingly, the ability to do so is least available within management and executives ranks, CIOs (unfortunately) included.

After studying the actions of great CIOs and talking to them at length, we found that they follow a clearly defined process to inspire people. It begins with the understanding of what we just talked about: that success can only come if people *want* to go in the direction you want them to. That means you need to establish a collaborative vision, so that people feel part of it, and then you must manage and maintain it to make sure people stay on course. With the vision firmly established, you nurture it by motivating people all around you to fulfill it by educating, encouraging, and lending support, and then you build great teams to execute it.

Let's see how this plays out in practice, starting at the beginning with the understanding that leaders who have no one behind them are not leaders at all. That, as Ramón Baez, CIO of Kimberly-Clark, told us, is a pivotal insight. "The turning point in my career was when I acknowledged, if I'm ever going to move up the corporate ladder, I've got to get people to *want* to go in the direction I think they should go."[5]

Pavitt tells a great story that makes the point:

If you go into the English countryside, you can see one man and his dog driving sheep where he wants them to go. These are very skillful sheepdogs, who run all around the flock, nip at the sheep's heels if they need to, and get the sheep to go where the shepherd wants them to go.

A POTENTIALLY TROUBLING QUESTION

Do you truly know your people are behind you 100 percent, or do you find yourself looking over your shoulder to check to see if they are following? Do you do all the selling of your vision, or have you inspired others to the point where they do the talking for you?

But if you visit the Middle East, you'll find that the shepherds are out in the front and the sheep are following. There is no dog.

Now, sheep are sheep. But somehow, Middle Eastern sheep have recognized that they don't need a dog to drive them. They say about the shepherd, "This guy looks after me; I will follow him."

In the U.K., we need a dog to drive them, and most leadership, unfortunately, works the same way. We keep nipping at people's heels to get them to follow us. I try to lead from the front, and because of the way I have explained things and the ways I have treated them, people say, "You know what? I like him," or "I like what he stands for, and I will follow him." I strive to get to that point as quickly as I can.

CONSTRUCTING THE COLLABORATIVE VISION

In creating your vision, the one designed to compel action, where do you start? The counterintuitive answer to "Where do we start?" is "At the end."

"We set the goal of what we want to accomplish; we describe what success will look like, and then we work backwards from there," says Filippo Passerini, president, global business services and CIO of Procter & Gamble. "We never say, 'Here is where we are now. What can we do going forward?' Rather, we begin by imaging what success will look like."[6] (For a more detailed look at how P&G goes about doing that, see "How P&G's IT Department Goes About Creating a Vision.")

HOW P&G'S IT DEPARTMENT GOES ABOUT CREATING A VISION

"Creating our vision always starts with us asking what are the megatrends in the world's markets that are affecting our business," says Filippo Passerini. "From there, we ask which of them are relevant to P&G.

"We ask what can we uniquely influence, and finally, we focus on the technologies that will deliver the biggest breakthrough. This is the four-step sequence that we always follow."

That sequence led to the IT department's current vision:

1. Drive global scale, standardization, and partnerships to deliver better services, lower costs, and greater agility.

2. Leverage IT, shared services, and process innovation to drive sustainable top- and bottom-line growth.

3. Unleash P&G's ability to digitize, visualize, and simulate.

Passerini then gave an example, dealing with the third part of the vision, that shows how this plays out in practice:

One trend that we believe is here to stay is acceleration of innovation to market. You've seen that in any number of sectors. In the automotive industry, it used to take five or six years to produce a new model. Now, the most agile companies are down to about twelve to fifteen months. Consumer electronics is moving even faster. This trend is obviously also affecting P&G.

From an information technology point, we thought we could influence the trend and play a leadership role. Here's one example of what we did: We used to hold consumer focus groups where we would show people physical mock-ups of our products. We'd listen to their feedback about artwork, packaging, colors, and the like, and then redo the mock-ups to incorporate their comments. It took about four to six weeks to make all the changes. Then we'd show a new group of consumers the improvements, listen to what they had to say, and go off and redo everything again.

Now, we do it using virtual reality. Instead of creating physical mock-ups, we now create virtual ones. This allows us to test the same products, colors, and packaging—only much faster. Processes that used to take weeks now take days or hours. And we can iterate much faster too. So we innovate faster and better, and we speed time to market too.

It is clear from our interviews with leading CIOs that the best visions have two parts. The first part ties to the overall corporate mission and objectives. For example, Tim Zoph needs to explain to his people how Northwestern Memorial Hospital's mission that "patients come first in all we do" relates to how his people should do their job. He needs to show them why the organization's belief that "whether we're involved directly in patient care or not, every employee of Northwestern Memorial Hospital can impact the quality of the patient experience and the level of excellence we collectively achieve" is true for them.[7]

Says Zoph, "I want to tie everything I do back to the core mission of the hospital; I want people to feel connected to it. So, whether we are constructing buildings, whether we are evolving

---

Great CIOs communicate a compelling vision, one that inspires others to get the right things done and the organization to perform at a higher level. A vision that doesn't lead to desired actions is just a waste of time.

electronic medical records, or making fundamental changes so that technology enabled processes are run with more precision, I want people to know what we are doing makes a difference in the care and treatment of our patients. The more my staff understands how what we do every day affects the patients, the more motivated, the more inspired they are going to be."

As Phil Pavitt underscores, "people can become skeptical about big visions. You need to impact things that they live with every day." The second part of creating your vision is equally—if not more—important. You explain to people how the vision will involve them in something greater than themselves. For example, Zoph's people know they are modeling what health care can become on behalf of their patients.

Ideally, the two parts—how the vision fits with the corporate objectives and how your people are personally affected by the vision—are combined into one memorable idea. A great example of a vision statement that achieves this goal is when Steve Jobs said Apple would build "insanely great products." This statement vividly explained the company's objective, let the employees know that incremental improvements were not the goal, and explicitly told employees that if they succeeded, they would be part of something that fundamentally changed the impact of technology on people's lives.

Did Jobs's vision work? You don't have to look any further than the iPod, the iPhone, and Pixar films to see that it did.

But that, Richard Gius argues, is not surprising: "When you can leverage the passion that is inside everyone who works with you by creating an inspiring vision, you can achieve great things." That was a message we heard constantly. "It is passion and enthusiasm that drive people to achieve higher levels of performance," says Rick Chapman, CIO of Kindred Healthcare. "We, as leaders, can inspire and nurture that passion or snuff it out."

The people on the receiving end of a great vision agree. Karen Nocket of Toyota speaks about her boss, Barbra Cooper: "She paints a picture of the future that is so attractive that you want to do it with her. I don't know too many CIOs

As we studied high-performing CIOs, we were not surprised to learn they had a compelling vision. What distinguished them was that their vision often went far beyond the walls of IT and often beyond the walls of the company. They consistently tried to have an impact on the customer and the industry.

who have that gift. Maybe most of them are really good managers, but Barbra's definitely in the category of a leader."[8]

But the kind of inspiration Nocket is talking about should *not* be limited solely to your organization. "Since we outsource, it's important that I get our outsourcers just as excited about Kimberly-Clark as I do the people within our company," says Ramón Baez. "If I don't, it's going to be very hard to influence them to go in the direction we need to head."

INSPIRING: MOVING FROM VISION TO EXECUTION

The question remains, though, how do high performers *inspire* others to follow, to execute? This is a vital skill—as we have said, it is one of the top three correlated with superior performance—yet is lacking among most executives, including CIOs. Still, the best CIOs are able to work through others and encourage them to share in fulfilling this vision. How do these CIOs do it?

It begins by forging a connection. In interviewing people for this book, we repeatedly found that the best CIOs had an incredible way of connecting to people. This is possible because of their highly social-participative leadership style, as we saw in chapter 2, and their highly developed interpersonal skills, as noted in chapter 3. And it all comes together in such a way that people feel the CIO genuinely cares about them as a person.

With the connection in place, the best CIOs inspire others by excelling at managing the vision and purpose, motivating, and building effective teams.

MANAGING THE VISION AND PURPOSE

The best CIOs understand that as important as a vision or strategy may be, effectively *communicating it and managing it is even more critical.*

Initially, most of us think in broad, sweeping terms when we hear the word *vision*—things like "I believe that this nation should commit itself to achieving the goal, before this decade is out, of landing a man on the moon and returning him safely to earth," or Martin Luther King's "I have a dream" speech.[9]

However, visions need not be that bold. So while the vision doesn't have to be grand, it does need to reflect the situational context of the enterprise. More specifically, it needs to create a compelling picture of the future, talk about possibilities, and be something that everyone can participate in—providing excellent customer service, for example—if it is to inspire and motivate others.

"There are some situations that call for rah-rah speeches and people like that," says Gius. "Most of the time, though, I think people just want to understand why something is important and how it contributes to the success of the organization."

The best CIOs, we found, provide the appropriate context. Every one of their direct reports—and the direct reports of their direct reports—could explain exactly where what they do fits within the company's overall vision and objectives.

And that is certainly true if you are introducing a radical new picture of the future. Once you get everyone fired up about it, you have to keep your people on course to make sure they accomplish it.

It's just as important to effectively communicate and manage a
vision as it is to have a vision.

Dean Harrison, president and CEO of Northwestern Memorial Hospital, is a great example of that. "We work hard to make sure we have a strategic vision and plan that align with our mission and motivate our organization toward success," he says. "One of our core strengths is how we apply rigorous standards and accountability toward achievement of our vision. We have a clear destination in mind and a proven process for getting there. However, we do allow for some fluidity on our planning so that we can take advantage of opportunities that may help accelerate our journey."[10]

Randy Spratt, chief technology officer of McKesson, underscores the counterintuitive notion that part of managing your vision is the understanding that it may evolve. "If you orient your goals and plans toward continuous improvement, instead of punishing failure," says Spratt, "then you begin to build an environment of accountability and an environment of improvement rather than the more negative outcomes."[11]

Indeed, a core part of managing the vision is the recognition that it is a work in progress, something to be refined over time to remain relevant, as marketplace conditions and the needs of the enterprise change. The best leaders know—and communicate to their people—that their vision is a living idea, one that will evolve over time.

The takeaway from this section is clear: managing the vision (keeping people focused on your goal) is critical because (1) you have to get people to take action and (2) you need to know that they are taking the right actions, the ones in alignment with the vision.

MOTIVATING OTHERS

High performers are also great motivators because they believe that everyone brings something different to the table. They assess those differences and use them effectively to get the best out of the individual and the team. They communicate, offer help, ask for help, walk the talk, and respect the individual.

You can see all that in the way they construct the vision itself. Drawing on their social-participative leadership styles, they create a collaborative vision. They don't dictate what the future should look like in isolation. They get key people to contribute. For example, Sony CIO Shinji Hasejima gives his high-potential direct reports the task of developing strategy because they will be the people who will ultimately need to make it a reality.

You need to take this approach if you want to make sure your vision is both the best it can be and able to be fulfilled. To make both of those things happen means, of course, that you need to motivate the people who work with you to give it their all.

Ramón Baez of Kimberly-Clark points out that the easiest way to make that happen is by changing the typical relationship between boss and employee: "The leaders of the past felt like they should be served instead of serving. No employee likes that. But they sure like to work for somebody who says, 'Hey, can I help you with that problem you are having?' So, my job is to help employees break obstacles they face."

Spratt makes a similar point: "Unless you are continuously influencing the day-to-day lives of the employees who are on the ground interacting with customers every day, you're not going to have the ability to deliver." But not only do you have to be there to motivate, you also need to be consistent—your commitment to making the vision a reality can't waiver—and you need to be authentic.

Let's take those points one at a time. People need to know where you stand. That means you need to know where you stand. It is vitally important that you are crystal clear not only on your vision, but also on your personal values—the things you believe—and what your professional values are. (What will get someone fired? What will get him or her promoted? What will you do to close a deal? What won't you? What would cause you to quit?)

Everyone wants to work in a place where the leader and the organization itself stand for something the person believes in.

And once you know what you stand for, your actions must be absolutely consistent with those beliefs. People want their leaders to have the courage to stand up for their convictions and not take the easy way out.

As one person who has seen Baez in action says, "What I like most about Ramón, even more than his energy level, is that he is very direct. He doesn't play games. There's no calculating; you're never wondering if what he says is what he really means. It's straightforward. It's honest; it's trustworthy. Employees like that. His peers like that. I like that."

All this is important because people are never motivated by people they don't trust, and if there is a disconnect between what you say is important and how you act, they won't trust you. You must live your values every day.

Gius tells a wonderful story about the payoff that can come from that:

When I was CIO at Allegiance, we had a huge project. And for a number of people on my staff, it was going to mean working sixty hours a week for an extended period of time. I didn't like asking people to do it. I think that is really, really disruptive to them and their families. It's a sure-fire way to burn people out and to lose great employees. But we were faced with a competitive deadline, and if we didn't get this done, there would be huge negative consequences for the corporation.

I spent a lot of time with my team making sure they understood that, but more importantly, I was passionate about all the positive things that would happen to the company if we got it done and how the rest of the company really would see us as heroes. And I told them that once it was done (which it was, on time and on budget), [they should] take some time off to decompress and spend time with their families or whatever. So the passion was not only about getting things done; my passion is around my support for my team, my commitment to them. I may be critical of some of the things they do, but they never have to worry about my support for them.

BUILDING EFFECTIVE TEAMS

Great CIOs believe that the whole really is greater than the sum of the parts. Consequently, these leaders create strong team spirit, dedicate time to removing team roadblocks, and define success in terms of the team.

"At the start of each fiscal year, I like to send out a set of objectives that the team collectively works towards," says Sherry Aaholm of FedEx. "But those objectives aren't something that I make up on my own. They're a collective set of objectives between me and the team." Aaholm says that if the team members are engaged, they'll feel accountable for the objectives, instead of feeling as if the goals are just her objectives. "This way, they're our objectives, the things *we* need to get done."

One reason the best leaders put in all this effort is because they know everyone wants to be part of a winning team. "People want to work for a company, or a department within a company, and a leader who is successful, so they can be proud of what they're doing and can go on at length to their friends and families about the place they work, because it makes them look and feel good," says Rick Chapman, CIO and chief administrative officer of Kindred Healthcare.[12]

And because people like to be part of a winning team, the best leaders not only let everyone know when they are doing a good job, but also passionately reward the right behaviors, modeling the actions they want in the process. That's why, for example, the best CIOs celebrate wins as part of their overall strategy to build momentum.

"You want to do that in front of the entire company if you can, and certainly in front of the entire IT department," says Chapman. Again, leaders do this with all their stakeholders, not just the immediate members of the organization, because they understand it is vitally important to motivate and inspire everyone.

And, when building a great team, CIOs often take on the hardest tasks—such as negotiating with all the parties involved to come up with a plan that will allow the team to execute the vision. They troubleshoot. They have the painful conversations when someone is underperforming or not living up to the team's standards. They don't shy from addressing business partners who are not aligned. They do all this both to make sure the team succeeds, and to show that they, themselves, are a fully committed part of the team.

RECOGNIZING THAT THE BAR IS NOW RAISED

As P&G's Passerini was quick to stress to us, inspiring others is not easy today:

> Managing your own organization, when you have power over salary increases, career promotions, and so forth, is a relatively simple model. What is less simple is the place we find ourselves today, where you manage in a network-dependent world. Yes, you have contracts with your partners in place, but the reality is you have less control. As a result, leading is more complex, but it is much more rewarding too. An organization that is truly best in class is an organization that is creating an environment for individuals to be better than they'd be on their own. Not only is it operating at a higher level, causing the individual to do better work, it is creating opportunities for them to

FIGURE 6-1

Inspiring by using vision, managing purpose, and building teams harnesses people's passions

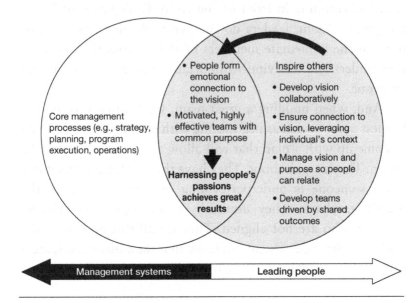

grow. So we constantly need to explain to people why the course of action we want to follow is not only good for the business, but good for the organization and good for them. I always tell our people they will grow and develop much, much faster if they operate in this world.

You can see the benefits of inspiring others in figure 6-1.

CALL TO ACTION

If you are still looking back to see if others are following, consider the following tips for development:

ASK YOURSELF, "DOES MY VISION MATTER?" Is your "vision" just an idea you happen to think is cool, or does it really have an impact that gets others feeling excited and compelled to action? Why should anyone care? Does it drive business results for the entire organization (and possibly beyond) or just IT?

PREPARE FOR A BUMPY ROAD. When leaders encounter indifference or pushback to their attempts to promote their vision, they often say to themselves, "But I didn't really mean it like that." Avoid the "oops, I didn't mean it like that" phenomenon by taking time before opening your mouth (or putting pen to paper) to think through all the things that might go awry with trying to deliver your message and inspire others. This might not help you avoid all the potholes in the road, but it will at least make the ride a bit smoother. You might even decide, after a more careful analysis, to choose a new road altogether.

PUT THE "OUR" IN YOUR VISION. When you've got a great idea, don't keep it to yourself. In fact, the earlier you get it out there (especially before it has become fixed in your mind) and the wider a circle of input you invite, the richer and more robust your vision becomes. In the process, you are also setting the stage for inspiring others because their ideas and perspective are adding to the whole and making it greater than the sum of its parts.

GIVE EVERYONE A ROLE TO PLAY. Everyone should play a part in making the vision a reality. Everyone. Even the people who showed some hesitancy at first or are even outright detractors. Working alongside others to build and execute the vision slowly but surely draws each person into something larger than himself or herself and strengthens the team. By giving everyone a role to play, you can also stand up at the end and truly say that everyone played a part and that it was a true team effort. By going further and recognizing each person's individual contribution, you provide important feedback that reinforces motivation and drives future performance.

SUMMING UP

As you have seen throughout, the only way we can truly get work done and achieve great results is with others. (There is only so much we can accomplish on our own.) That means we must get people to follow where we want to lead.

And while many a general business book has been written on the development of a vision and inspiration as it relates to leading, CIOs are in a unique spot. Given both your role and the combined impacts of globalization, hyperconnectivity, and rapid shifts in the business and technological environments, you are challenged to create and manage a vision that reaches well beyond the walls of your organization.

So the first part of that vision that you need to create, if it is going to be effective, invariably ties to the organization's goals and objectives. The second part gets people to believe in something larger than themselves.

Creating the vision isn't enough. To actually achieve something of significant and lasting value, it is just as important to communicate and manage the vision in a way that inspires others and makes things happen.

The CIOs who do this best draw upon several related skills to lead others beyond what they initially thought possible. They manage vision and purpose in a way that clarifies for others what actions need to be taken to align with and accomplish the vision. They lead and motivate others by continuously staying involved and by honestly, clearly, and consistently communicating their values. And they build effective teams with a winning attitude, where everyone, the CIO included, is accountable for the team's success.

The result is a more cohesive, effective enterprise, one where people not only enjoy, but also are energized by, coming to work. And the work is accomplished more easily since everyone—both inside the organization and out—knows that he or she is not only creating value but also shaping a better future.

BUILD PEOPLE, NOT SYSTEMS

INCREASE CAPABILITY AND CAPACITY
TO DELIVER RESULTS

Gerald Shields, CIO of Aflac, the large insurance company, vividly recalls the "aha" moment, a specific day in April 1997, when he realized his role needed to fundamentally change. It came after IT finished—on time and on budget—a huge, complicated project. The group had relentlessly driven to the goal and brought it across the finish line, albeit via a "death march" of continuously long days—that ended well into the night—and weekend after weekend of work.

> *Once we were done, I looked around and realized that there was no one around to celebrate with me. By the time we had gotten to the end, I had killed the troops. Everyone had gone off to take some—or a lot—of time off to recover. Some ultimately chose to leave the company and, ultimately, the IT profession altogether. It was a hollow victory. Not because I thought I had done*

anything wrong. We had to get the job done by a specific date, and we had. But because there was no one there to high-five when we succeeded. They were all home in bed exhausted.

I thought about that a lot, and after a great deal of soul-searching, I concluded that I had built my last system. I had been a pretty good systems person. I'd been very successful in designing and building applications. But after thinking back on this project, I came to the conclusion that I was going to fundamentally redefine my role. I was going to take the same passion, the same determination, the same skill set that allowed me to build systems, and I was going to use it to build people. From that moment on, I looked at my job as building the very best IT professionals.

Why? First, it is the most effective way to create value and sustained impact for the organization. It is the way to make the biggest difference. Everyone has access to the same technology. It is what you do with it that makes the difference. And it is people who decide how that technology is deployed effectively.

Second, I wanted the people who worked for me to say, "I accomplished more in my career because I worked in Gerald's organization and because of what he invested in me."

I was totally convinced that the combination of those two things would have the highest impact for the enterprise, would be best for my people, and would be the most productive and fulfilling way for me to spend my time. And it turns out I was right.[1]

THOSE WHO DON'T fully come to this realization (i.e., those who have not had an "aha" moment as Shields did) can become trapped in a futile cycle of trying to be everywhere, trying to keep up with the relentless demands, constantly plugging the holes in the dike, and feeling increasingly burned out. As a result, they end up frustrated with the others around them as they work desperately hard merely to stay even with the increasing demands of their job.

Conversely, if you develop your people, you can get far more work done via others, achieve far greater success, and drive more value from IT. You also increase your job satisfaction, the best CIOs told us, because watching someone flourish because of your own efforts is immensely fulfilling.

That's why the highest performers invest what to the average CIO seems like a disproportionate amount of time, energy, and passion in developing people. These high performers know that it will be a leading indicator of future performance and departmental (and company) success.

As Barbra Cooper, CIO of Toyota, told us, "If I had to write a one-sentence descriptor of what is expected of a high-performing CIO, I would say, 'Your responsibility as a leader is to develop the next generation of leaders.' Besides, if you don't do it, there is no way the organization is going to survive long term."[2]

CIOs like Cooper consider people development a core responsibility and not a "nice to have," or ancillary, part of their job.

DEVELOPING PEOPLE EVERYWHERE IN THE ORGANIZATION

The best CIOs understand that developing people is not limited to their direct reports, but just as importantly (if not more so)

The best CIOs possess an extreme passion for developing talent and the next generation of business technology leaders.

---

extends to key stakeholders such as their peers, business partners, and even their boss and board of directors. As Tim Zoph, CIO of Northwestern Memorial Hospital, puts it:

> Our ultimate role should be to be the supplier of talent for the organization. IT is unique in the visibility it has across the business. Our view is second to none, since we are involved in just about every operation. The collateral effect of that is we have the opportunity to grow both the technical literacy of our stakeholders and their confidence in what the technology can do. That's important because I want to have the organization embrace technology to drive change.
>
> Let me explain. The real limiting factor for effective use of technology is the combination of literacy and confidence from the rest of the business. That's why I think a principal role of the CIO leader of the future will be cultivating technological literacy through the breadth and depth of the organization.[3]

And the only way he can achieve that literacy is to build the technology capabilities of everyone organizationwide. No, people don't need to know how to write code or implement a major system upgrade, but they do need—as Cooper told us— "more than a passing knowledge of what the technology is— and is not—capable of." Educating them about that is a vital

---

A POTENTIALLY UNSETTLING QUESTION

The ultimate success of the CIO comes from how well her people perform.

And that raises this troubling thought: do you make the needed investments in your people to enable them to perform to their highest potential?

---

part of your job. Because this idea is so important, we will return to it later in the chapter.

DEVELOPING SELF-AWARENESS FIRST

So how do you go about building your people? Intriguingly, the best place to start is by building yourself.

Although the high-performing leaders whom we interviewed already possessed and used with great success strong leadership qualities, they were also acutely self-aware. Not only are they more reflective of their own performance and actions (e.g., the way they communicate and behave in a crisis) and the shadow they cast as a leader, but they are critically more attuned to how others perceive them.

Not surprisingly, then, they are open and more "feedback friendly." When given feedback, they see it as an opportunity to improve, rather than denying the comments or trying to explain away the critique. They see feedback—even when it is negative—as part of a process of lifetime learning, understanding that once you are satisfied with where you are, the universe will pass you by.

"The only way to really find out how effective you are as a leader," says Zoph, "is to be willing to listen to others about your own leadership, and be able to take feedback constructively, and be able to fine-tune your leadership style based on the perception of others."

By committing to self-improvement, these leaders are doing three things simultaneously:

1. *Bettering themselves.* They are gaining the skills and knowledge that will allow them to be more successful. As Shields puts it, "self-awareness is the number one key to performance. If I could change anything in people, I would try to make them be more self-aware."

2. *Modeling the behavior they want.* It is not enough for you to want to develop your people; your people must

want to improve. By showing that you, their boss, are committed to getting better, you make it easier for them to embrace a course of personal development as well.

3. *Making themselves vulnerable.* High-performing leaders are saying to their staff, "I don't know everything," which in turn can help employees own up to their own weaknesses.

Robert Runcie, chief administrative officer, formerly CIO, of Chicago Public Schools, serves as a case in point:

I started 360 reviews about three years ago. I took mine and handed it to my direct reports. While a couple of them had been involved in giving feedback about me, as part of my 360, the vast majority of them hadn't. So, I gathered my entire team, gave them my 360 report, and told them I wanted to get feedback about my performance from them. Then I left the room and went out to lunch with another department head, so they could feel comfortable discussing it. When I came back ninety minutes later, I got some really great feedback from them on what I did well and things they thought I may want to change, things like how to get them to work better as a team.

Why did I have them do it? Well, first, of course, because I want to get better. But if I want the directors who work for me to begin to have that kind of dialogue within their own department, then I need to demonstrate the skill, the ability to be open to getting that kind of feedback. The only way they're going to get better is if they have these kinds of conversations with their peers and their staff.

If people can acknowledge the weaknesses and challenges they have, the people they work with can help them get better, which will, in turn, make the organization better.[4]

As we have seen, it is within the context and experience of their own self-awareness and personal development journey that the highest performers create the foundation on which they can best develop others, for the more self-aware and self-confident you are, the greater capacity and role modeling of leadership you can offer.

BUILDING THE NEXT GENERATION OF IT LEADERS

As we said, the primary sustainable lever to pull in shaping the future is building others. Why? Because when it is done well, it not only expands your sphere of influence (increasing both the capacity and speed at which you can enable change) but does so in a way that will endure even when you are not there.

The question is how you do it. The Lominger research confirmed for us something that we found in our interviews with high-performing CIOs. The most effective way to develop people falls into three large (and disproportionate) categories.

- 70 percent comes from experiential learning and from stretch or rotational assignments.

- 20 percent occurs through coaching and mentoring.

- 10 percent comes about through traditional learning (courses, etc.).[5]

Let's walk through each of the components one at a time.

OFFERING EXPERIENCE, THE BEST TEACHER

The best CIOs repeatedly told us that their own stretch and rotational assignments—being put in positions where they got on-the-job learning—were the biggest factor in their development as leaders. That could explain why they are such huge advocates of giving their direct reports the same experiences.

For example, Toyota's Barbra Cooper recognized early that Karen Nocket had the ability to be a CIO herself one day. To help her realize that potential, Cooper mapped a ten-year development plan for Nocket. The plan included a stretch assignment whose primary purpose was to give Nocket a much better understanding of supply-chain dynamics and made sure she was thrust into high-pressure situations throughout the company.

With Cooper's coaching, Nocket has learned how to communicate effectively how IT could not only help, but add value, using terms, concepts, and thinking that everyone else in the organization could relate to and ultimately embrace. And along the way, Nocket succeeded in building collaborative executive business partner relationships—no small feat.

"Every month," says Nocket, "I have an hour-plus with Barbra one-on-one (and if I need more, I get more). I don't use it as a status meeting ('here's where I am on this particular project'). I use the time so that she can coach, rather than manage me. In addition, Barbra has made sure I have supplemented my learning with leadership courses at UCLA and USC. And I have done a couple at Harvard and MIT."[6]

What has Nocket learned from all this? "Our greatest challenge is the pace of change and the relentless demands of our business partners. And I really hadn't counted on knowing how important it is to actually develop my people, and how much time that I spend on a weekly basis doing that. I can't directly touch the $200 million worth of work I am responsible for; it's impossible. But if I give opportunities to the high potentials who work for me to stretch beyond what they think they're capable of doing, I can help build a high-performing team. I feel a responsibility to do that. Because Barbra's work doesn't stop with me."

Has this development worked? Perhaps too well. Cooper has had two of her peers who head different parts of the company come to her to ask if they could hire Nocket to run various parts of their departments.

If you left the office for an extended period (or left altogether),
would your people be sufficiently developed to lead in your
absence? If not, what are you doing to change that?

ROTATING

A variation on offering people more experience is to give them rotational assignments. For example, you can send members of your IT staff to work on the business side of the organization for an extended period—six months to two years is typical. Sherry Aaholm of FedEx has her high potentials do regular rotations, including extended periods overseas, in various business units throughout the company, to make sure that IT can support the company's global business model.

P&G has its high performers spend time working in other parts of the business, and even has rotations where people spend up to twelve months, working in roles within the company's key vendors to help these leaders form even closer relationships with suppliers. These kinds of rotations are a simple and effective way for your staff not only to gain a better understanding of both how the organization serves customers and makes money, but also to learn how IT contributes and adds value. The only way to truly understand the challenges people in the rest of the organization face is, as the cliché says, to walk in their shoes.

One important point: everyone knows that rotational assignments are useful. Everyone knows that we need to build literacy. What's different about the examples we just read is that it was actually getting done. The IT people do it, *and* the business people do it.

And that is the bigger point. We all know that this is what we are supposed to do, but only a few actually *do* it. The best leaders have developed the credibility in the organization to make it

Essentially, development is the land of the first time and the difficult. Comfortable circumstances and applying skills we already have does not lead to growth. In fact, it leads to stagnation. Lack of challenge also prompts talented people to look for another employer.

happen. They are able to execute because they have developed people, built relationships, and got work done through others.

Again, this is consistent with how the best CIOs learned themselves. According to the Lominger research, some 75 to 90 percent of learning occurs on the job. More specifically, most of the hard job skills that matter most for performance are learned on the job when people hit fresh challenges. The jobs that are least likely to teach are straight upward promotions, doing the same type of job again and again, and job switches aimed merely at exposure rather than tough challenges.

COACHING AND MENTORING

The second tool the best CIOs use to develop their people is coaching and mentoring. Shields, for example, spends three hours a week—there are dedicated periods on Monday and Wednesday—doing so.

He describes some typical activities: "I facilitate sessions that are open to all people who are in leadership positions within the department. That would be the supervisors over computer operations, the supervisors over the desktop support team, all the way up to my vice presidents. We'll take a leadership book and go through that. Or I will tell them about a situation I had where I screwed it up, and what I learned from doing so and what I am doing differently as a result. We will talk through different situations and discuss what approaches to take."

Of course, coaching doesn't have to be a formally scheduled activity. The day-to-day interactions of the CIO with direct reports and others provide many opportunities for "coachable moments." As P&G's Filippo Passerini says, "people development is a cumulative thing. There isn't one silver bullet. We don't say, 'Go there, or do this, and you will become a better leader,' although we do have many formal programs and classes. There is a constant conversation and dialogue. Every interaction is an opportunity for two-way learning. I can learn something, and so can the person I am dealing with."[7]

But no matter how you do coaching and mentoring, you have to do it. As Cooper says, "it's a matter of survival. If you don't do it, you aren't going to have many options going forward. The converse is that an emphasis on people development equals high value creation."

The kinds of skills you should teach will depend on what you think the universe will look like going forward. "I spend an inordinate amount of time readying my team's competencies in the areas that they are going to need over the next fifteen years," Cooper explains by way of example:

> You can't wait until you actually need them. It takes a while for people to learn and develop. My list of what future competencies we focus on developing is still evolving, but they center around business acumen— understanding economics, understanding the organizational development techniques, talent management (and I am pleased to see that my direct reports have begun spending a lot of time developing their own teams), how to build a business case that is legit, and so on— combined with the ability to influence. That's why, as we have said throughout, going forward, you'll need a higher level of consultative communication and strong influencing skills, in addition to your understanding of technology.

This kind of education is appreciated by Cooper's direct reports, who are quick to stress that its need came as a surprise. Says Nocket:

> We went to school to learn how to program and how to design. Nobody taught us that we also should have been taking psychology, and communications, and writing, and speech-giving, and politics. That was not in my job description when I signed on. Nor was I taught that in school, and yet obviously, it is vital. Barbra has staged the next couple of jobs for me so I can learn more of these things. I'm on a ten-year journey that she has planned for me that will take me from a technical manager to a divisional CIO. She constantly moves the bar on you and will talk about things I'll need to know two years from now. And sometimes you think your head is going to explode, but you understand what she is saying, because she has built the foundation, and she makes it clear why what she is teaching is important.

What is often forgotten is that coaching forces you to determine what you think is important and worth passing on. "You learn a lot from teaching," Zoph said. "You learn about your own leadership style. You learn what's important to you. The act of teaching is in itself a way to center your message and distill your thoughts."

So, teaching helps the best CIOs refine their own values and philosophies, helping them improve as leaders. This is another example of how working to develop others has the very pleasant by-product of helping you to improve yourself, something that Carol Zierhoffer, CIO of ITT, understands. "I tend to lean towards developing very, very strong relationships downward, with the people that work for me. It's a key part of my leadership style. I'm there to make them successful, and therefore I become successful."

Developing the next generation of leaders is a three-part process. The person needs to be ambitious and willing to do what's required to grow and progress. The organization must have a process in place to help those who want to grow. And the boss has to be an active player in the development, or it won't happen.

It is in this last part where organizations (and leaders) run into trouble. Without the boss's time, interest, and effort, people will not grow much. People can't develop themselves fully without some formal or informal help from others. People won't realize their potential if you don't make it a priority.

Between teaching, coaching, and mentoring, Barbra Cooper estimates that she spends 30 to 40 percent of her time in those people development areas. "CIOs work really hard, and we try to stay educated and do the right things, but one of the areas where we fall down is that very few of us are taking enough time to teach, coach, and mentor," she says.

One reason this might be the case is that mentoring often involves having difficult conversations. Gerald Shields recalls one of the toughest ones he had:

After this person had worked for me for about eighteen months and just refused to get better in this one pivotal area, I really had a heart-to-heart with them. I said, "Here are the areas where you are strong, and you know what they are. And here's where you are weak, and you know that, too. And I want to tell you something plainly so you understand it. When I fire you, it's gonna be the most difficult thing I will have had to do in my career. I dread that day, because you are so talented that you could be the most talented person I have ever terminated."

And this person literally started crying when they heard that. I said, "OK, here's the way to keep that from happening." And we went through it step by step. I told them, "I will do everything I can to help you do your job, but I can't do your job for you. And I can't spend time going back behind you doing clean-up work." They took the message to heart. They are well on the way to being a CIO.

What is clear from all this is that people won't grow if you don't make their growth a priority. People can't fully develop themselves without help.

But the onus is not entirely on you. The people you are developing must want to get better as well and commit to the hard work and sacrifice that development requires. They must understand where they need to develop and must feel motivated to get better. They need to embrace the stretch assignments and the coaching, take advantage of the courses you recommend, and do reading (and questioning) on their own.

Your best employees will understand that. "Of course, our employees want P&G to be successful," Passerini says. "But I think it is inevitable for human beings to also think about 'what's in it for me?' And what's in it for the people is two things. First, your job becomes much more interesting, because we are exposing you to many more things, and second, you grow professionally disproportionately more than you would do otherwise."

DEVELOPING IT LITERACY ACROSS
THE ENTERPRISE

The highest-performing CIOs have a passion for building the people all around them—their peers (key horizontal relationships), the people above them (their boss and the board), and even other stakeholders (suppliers and other important partners). The way that Toyota does this works well. The company has future leaders, those it labels "high potentials," do a rotation through the IT department run by Barbra Cooper as part of their career path (just as you, as the CIO, have your people do rotational assignments outside IT as part of their development).

That is something that Sony CIO Shinji Hasejima believes is extremely important: "We need to get involved in developing the next generation of strategies and help change the mind-set when it comes to IT. Business/IT rotations are a great way to do that. That's why we not only send IT people to the business side, for a two- or three-year rotation so that they gain business skills, but we also have people from the business side rotate through IT so they understand what it is we do and what technology is capable of achieving for the business."[8]

But CIOs like Cooper and Hasejima do more than spend time with future leaders. They are constantly working with everyone in the C-suite, explaining what the technology is capable of.

When you are talking to the CEO, working to develop his or her technological understanding, you are the subject matter expert and the CEO is not. And you are not trying to bring this person up to your level of understanding. But you are trying to get the executive to the point where he or she understands where the major technology enabled levers are and how they are changing. Most importantly, you want the CEO to be able to separate the myths from reality regarding what technology can do to impact the performance of the enterprise. Your job is to help the CEO (and the board) understand what is important, so that you are all on the same page when making a major decision.

You are trying to pass on your technological savvy to build an organizationwide capability. You want to end up with a collaborative, high-performing team that can excel in visionary planning, make tough decisions, and implement technology-enabled change. That is the payoff, and why the need for educated, technology-literate relationships are so important.

As IT becomes more pervasive and more embedded into the fabric
of every part of the business, all leaders—independent of their
functional background and current role—need to learn not only
what IT is capable of, but also how to best harness its value. It's
your job as CIO to make sure that they do. Which individuals would
benefit from your developing their technology literacy?

LEAVING YOUR LEGACY: SUSTAINED
VALUE CREATION

One last point. Just about every CIO we talked to spoke passionately—unprompted and at great length—about how
developing people is the legacy that you leave. "I feel very
strongly that if you are a leader, you need to cultivate the next
generation of leadership," Zoph told us. "You know, there's
nothing better than to teach a new generation from the position of experience. I feel a leadership obligation to cultivate
that next generation through teaching, mentorship, and
involvement. What you're really leaving behind is the strength
of the team of people that you've recruited and developed, and
a culture that you've built. That's what lives after you are gone.
So, yes, your job as the leader is important, but your real
importance is establishing those foundations that can live on."

And the best CIOs told us about the immense feeling of
pride they get from doing that. "I remember back when I was
working for Honeywell, I came back to the States, and got a
phone call from the finance manager I used to work with,"
Ramón Baez, now CIO of Kimberly-Clark, recalls. "He said,
'You did a really good job here, because when you left, we
never even noticed it.' At first I was sort of insulted. How could
they not miss me? But later on, I realized what a great compli-
ment that was. He was saying I was so good at my job, that I

had built the IT machine up to where when I left, people didn't notice the difference."[9]

We began the chapter talking to Gerald Shields. Let's end it the same way, because he makes the point about legacy in a particularly vivid way: "When I left my previous employer, there were four people who could have taken over for me as CIO. That was my biggest accomplishment, not replacing twenty-seven systems, but being able to leave and say, 'Hey, you know what? You've got a tough decision because I don't know if you want to give my job to Dan or Kay or Jeff or Don.' They didn't even consider going outside to replace me."

Shields, like the other CIOs we mentioned in the chapter, had created a high-performing team, one that could deliver results via IT. As figure 7-1 shows, this allows IT to provide substantial value to the organization, not only today but going forward as well.

FIGURE 7-1

Developing people increases capability and capacity to deliver results . . . in ways that endure

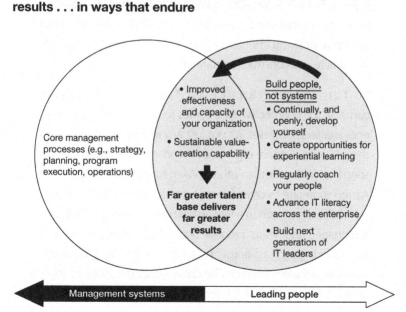

CALL TO ACTION

If you are still investing more in building systems than people, consider the following tips for development:

STEP UP AND COMMIT TO BUILDING PEOPLE. The first step is to admit you need to build people, and the next step is to commit to getting it done. Ask for help from human resources. If it doesn't have a formal succession planning process, do your own informally. Look across your calendar for the last few months, and be honest about the amount of time you spent in people-development activities. Then, commit to increasing it each month until you see that you are really having an impact.

GIVE TIMELY, DIRECT, AND SPECIFIC FEEDBACK. Sounds easy, but few excel at this. It comes down to a fundamental discomfort that most people have with delivering criticism. That's very understandable, but it's still no excuse. Think of it this way. How is someone going to get better if he or she is unaware of what needs to be addressed? That awareness begins with your drawing attention to the areas they need to develop in a timely and constructive manner.

MATCH THE EXPERIENCE TO THE NEED. As discussed earlier in the chapter, when it comes to development, experience matters. However, it's not just any experience that will get the job done. Certain experiences concentrate learning for specific skills better than others. Want to work on conflict? Assign someone to chair a cross-functional team. Motivating skills? Put the person in a leadership role with a team that is disengaged and needs a morale boost. Be creative and resourceful in making such assignments. If full-time assignments aren't available, consider what can be done within the scope of the person's current job role to stimulate development.

DELEGATE TO DEVELOP. The easiest form of delegation
is getting "busy work" off your plate. While this may do
wonders for your time management, it does correspondingly
little for the development of those who are being delegated
to do it. Remember, if it's not difficult, it's not developmental.
Pick assignments that provide novelty and challenge for the
individual and where the downside risk can be managed.
Then step back and give people some freedom to explore
and make choices on their own. If they come up short, treat
it as a learning experience.

REINFORCE THE LESSONS OF EXPERIENCE. The
right developmental opportunity and the right lessons can
go for naught if those lessons can't be applied to subsequent
experiences. Support awareness and application by helping
individuals to draw on the lessons they have learned from their
experiences and exploring how those insights can be applied
in other aspects of the job.

SUMMING UP

The highest-performing CIOs are devoted to, and passionate
about, developing the next generation of business technology
leaders. They model the behavior they want and work to make
sure their high-potential employees receive extensive experiential learning such as stretch projects and rotational assignments,
all supported by mentoring. These leaders embrace the role of
developing technology literacy across their enterprises.

Why do they do all this? Because if you focus on developing
your people to the fullest extent possible, four things happen, all
of them good:

You unleash the power of your organization. As you
know, it is neither a company's physical nor its financial

assets that provide true competitive advantage. It is the employees who use them. It is the organization's people who are the value-creation engine.

You increase the impact of IT. All that power within your people is capable of creating value and making extraordinary things happen for the organization. In other words, you broaden your ability to effect change from the CIO seat by developing, empowering, and getting results through others.

Your job becomes more fulfilling. While it is certainly satisfying to carry a technology project through to a successful completion, the CIOs we interviewed said they got more joy watching the people they were responsible for develop to their fullest potential and thrive as a result.

You build a sustainable legacy. Twenty-five years from now, no one in your organization is going to remember who was in charge of the major system upgrade of 2010. But the people running the technology department will remember the bosses who made a difference in their life. Your business partners will recall the person who helped them better exploit technology for business advantage. And the people you have trained and helped develop will have more of a lasting impact than any new system you install.

The result of all this is a dramatic increase in your capability and capacity to deliver results via technology—both today and well into the future. That's why you want to switch your primary focus to building people and not systems.

THE PROFESSIONAL PAYOFF: DELIVERING BUSINESS RESULTS

YOU GET TO MAXIMIZE IT VALUE—THE JOB YOU SIGNED UP TO DO

The amount of value that you as CIO can deliver is a function of your technology savvy and business acumen, unleashed and amplified by your people-leadership skills. But before you get to deliver maximum value, you have to just deliver. This was the case recently with the U.S. Postal Service (USPS). The USPS was going to do nothing less than radically overhaul the technology infrastructure that supported the way it monitored and managed information.

By the time the overhaul was done, not only would operations be streamlined, but a client would be able to track and analyze every single item it mailed. A credit card company, for example, would know in an instant if the check really was in the mail, as the customer said, and mail-order companies could learn exactly how long the interval was between the time customers received their catalog and placed an order, so the firm could adjust everything from call-center staffing levels to the amount of inventory it had in stock.

But there was a problem. The CIO was new; he had no industry experience and had been given just nine months to get everything done. (An aggressive deadline would have been two years.) In short, it was the most ambitious project the USPS had ever undertaken—and it had everything stacked against it.

But Ross Philo, the new CIO, was determined not only to deliver, but also to establish IT as a value provider. His approach: use IT for its technology knowledge; partner with Thomas G. Day, senior vice president of the USPS's Intelligent Mail business unit, to ensure business insight; and focus every ounce of personal energy on the people aspect of making it happen. Day recalls how things were going initially:

> You'd go into a meeting, and the moment a problem surfaced, all you heard was, "You didn't do this," and in response, "Oh yeah? Well, you didn't do that, and that is why we are in this mess."
>
> To stop that, we modified the organizational structure. We decided that Ross and I would cohead the project, and we created one integrated team. Then we said, "We collectively must make it happen. If we don't, then we are going to fail as a team."
>
> Every Wednesday, both the business and IT people charged with making the progress happen would meet to give updates. Bottlenecks and problems were identified, and people were assigned to fix them. We were typically correcting defects within forty-eight hours. So it was an unbelievable pace.[1]

Adds Philo:

> To keep that pace, we had to create and demonstrate a no-blame mentality. That didn't mean a laissez-faire attitude to mistakes, but rather recognizing they had

happened and we had a shared desire to overcome them. To use another analogy, we were all in the boat together, so everyone had a vested interest in plugging leaks as opposed to assessing blame.[2]

Day and Philo never missed an opportunity to reinforce a very clear and visible shared ownership by the business and IT. They held joint meetings, joint statements, joint celebrations. Says Day, "We often likened it to being a two-headed monster. But the key was to achieve a single body and a single thought, despite having two heads."

By providing constant communication in every direction—up to senior management, down throughout the organization, and sideways with vendors—and customizing it for each audience, Philo and Day were able to persuade their partners to live up to their commitments and deliver the necessary resources. And by repeatedly explaining the vision and historic scope to all involved, the two leaders got people to commit greater hours and more effort than they would to a run-of-the-mill initiative.

The project came in on time and on budget, with IT proving itself as a vital partner in value delivery.

So WHAT'S IN IT FOR YOU? What is the professional payoff from employing soft skills effectively? How does focusing on the seven people-leadership skills we have talked about enable you to create value for your enterprise and deliver on expectations, the things you are being judged on?

The answer is the *difference* between creating extraordinary value in collaborative partnership with business peers and just muddling along, trying to keep up with the relentless demands of the job. Employing people leadership (soft skills) effectively is what separates the great CIOs from the good ones. You saw that payoff at USPS in terms of ability to deliver. Later in the chapter, we will discuss an example of creating value via influencing strategy and shaping demand.

Clearly, you can have the same sort of impact, too, providing you combine soft skills, business acumen, and technological savvy in the right proportions. The key word in the preceding sentence is *combine*. Individually, technological savvy, business acumen, and soft skills are important, and each can be developed separately. But it is only when they are working together that a CIO can provide the maximum value to the enterprise. We call the melding of technological savvy, business acumen, and people skills (with the soft skills amplifying the first two) the *combinatorial advantage*.

Given what we just said, you might think that each of the three skills is of equal value, but it turns out that they are not. Our research shows that people skills are far and away the most important, followed by business acumen and technological savvy (assuming a threshold level of both). While improving skills in either or both business and technology is obviously helpful, the amount of leverage you can achieve is limited. So, given the choice of which skill to work on, the real payoff comes from honing superior leadership and interpersonal skills. When those people skills are combined with solid business and technical know-how, there is an amplification effect and the improvements are exponential, not arithmetic.

As one smart CIO told us, it is not until CIOs focus on people skills that they even have the opportunity to provide the greatest value: "It's the difference between picking the right CRM [customer relationship management] software, which any CIO can do, and delivering business results by changing the very nature of how the company looks at its customers."

The clear takeaway from this is that while many business leaders focus on their functional area of expertise, only the best look at their role through the prism of people. Ultimately, it is people who enable you to execute on any idea or vision in the marketplace. Let's see why this is the case. More specifically, let's explore the three areas you need to master and then illustrate why the combinatorial impact—especially if you lean most heavily on superior people skills—is, in this case, greater than the sum of its parts.

A POTENTIALLY TROUBLING QUESTION

If your goal is to join the ranks of the highest-performing CIOs and maximize IT value, not having superior people skills will make those goals extremely difficult, maybe impossible. Are you ready to embrace the challenge to make yourself a better leader?

TECHNOLOGICAL SAVVY

Technology is the primary tool you wield in the CIO role as an enabler and a source of value for your enterprise. Its ability to improve and indeed disrupt both business processes and business models alike moves forward unabated. Your technological savvy, the ability to understand the technology trends, distill what is truly meaningful, and capitalize on these shifts in combination with your team is a critical foundation for IT's value contribution.

First, you have to demonstrate your own technological competence and that of your team. That is something that Dave Swartz, CIO of American University (AU), learned:

> One of the first things I did when I came to AU was an ERP [enterprise resource planning] upgrade. Every time they did one in the past, it caused huge problems. The most recent one basically shut down the entire IT system for two months. So they were looking at this as something that was going to be nothing but painful for them. I showed them it didn't have to be. We applied the right project management techniques, made solid decisions on changes to the infrastructure, extensively tested everything, and so forth. Basically, we did the technology job, and did it well.

In fact, about two weeks after it was completed, I got a call from the registrar, asking when we were going to go live.

I said we went live two weeks ago.

Immediately after that, everybody on the campus, every dean and VP, the president called asking in shock, "You mean you did this without shutting down the university or having any major problems?"

I said, "Yeah, you just need to follow best practices." All of a sudden, I had a lot of trust with them, and they started asking us to do more and more.[3]

Sherry Aaholm of FedEx found the same thing to be true. Soon after she was named executive vice president for IT, she realized the company would significantly benefit if it could leverage more of its common solutions on a global basis. The problem? The regional presidents were used to controlling their own IT resources. Aaholm explains what happened:

Before I could seriously advocate for the kind of change I wanted, I needed to build up an element of trust with those partners first. I knew if I could demonstrate quick wins, they would begin to trust me and then I could start proposing more complicated things. So I would shift resources from one region to another, to help out someone who was struggling a bit, and I would introduce a piece of software that had worked elsewhere, to solve a specific problem someone else had, instead of building that solution twice, which would have been typical. I did four or five of those things, and by then, I had tremendous respect from business leaders to say, wow, they really can make things happen. So that gave me a little bit more of a sphere of influence on the business side and allowed me to start talking about some more difficult venues, such as their sales application.[4]

But even though you are the person at the center of figuring how the technology should best be employed, this does not mean you need to be the person in the organization who knows the most about it. "To be a successful CIO, you do have to have a strong IT acumen," says Carol Zierhoffer, CIO of ITT. "However, you don't necessarily have to have a deep understanding of everything. But your understanding must be wide. You need to be able to sniff out the b.s. But the job is so much more than understanding technology."[5]

Gerald Shields of Aflac believes the same thing: "Your troops don't have to believe you are the strongest technical person in the world, but they need to know you have a passion for the technology and the application of the technology and that you understand them."[6]

At first blush, it sounds counterintuitive to say that the *chief information officer* doesn't have to be the foremost authority on the technology, but it does make sense. If you leverage your people-leadership skills, making sure that you have true technology experts on staff, and more importantly, if you create the environment so that this expertise can be effectively applied, then you don't have to stay absolutely current on all the technology and details yourself. Indeed, trying to do this will distract you from your primary role as CIO: meeting expectations and maximizing value delivery.

BUSINESS ACUMEN

Going forward, the three skills you are going to need, in order, are convincing skills, understanding the business, and understanding the technology.
—Shinji Hasejima, CIO, Sony

Business acumen is an incredibly important trait to possess. There isn't anything you do in corporate IT that you can't buy somewhere else.
—Randy Spratt, CIO, McKesson

You need to be a good business leader first, and a technology leader second. I would say that you probably

need to spend somewhere around 60 percent of your time
on the business and, you know, 30 percent to 40 percent
dealing with IT-related matters.
—Robert Runcie, chief administrative officer,
Chicago Public Schools

The preceding quotations, comments the CIOs made during our interviews with them, are not an aberration. In countless interviews and workshops, the best CIOs told us that if, in order to do their job effectively, they were forced to choose between knowing more about business and knowing more about technology, they would choose business insights every time.

The point is not to have superior business knowledge in each function area (logistics, finance, marketing, etc.), but rather to know how all these things come together. In this way, you not only understand the business on a macro level, but also know where IT fits in and can contribute value. Marv Adams, former president of Fidelity Shared Services, is a big proponent of this approach:

I find that people often are stuck in their particular silo, like manufacturing or engineering, and they don't really see how what they do affects anyone else in the organization. One of the things I try to engrain in my organization is a systems-thinking orientation so that people see how all the pieces fit.

Say you make automobiles. If you don't take the time to design the optimal number of vehicle platforms, and you get sloppy and allow too many designs to come out of engineering, trying to be overly responsive to every little feature that sales wants, then you end up throwing so much variety into manufacturing that manufacturing can't possibly be efficient, and it affects their quality in a negative way.

IT is just one of those systems. You've got business demands that are either well thought out or they are not.

And if they aren't, they eventually create a hodgepodge of applications, and if the IT gets too overly driven by individual departments or businesses, they'll even build it on separate operating system and hardware platforms. That then flows through into the data centers, which then can't possibly be managed efficiently. But it really has nothing to do with anything that the data center did wrong. It has to do with not getting things engineered from the very first boundary in the most effective way.

So I put a lot of energy into trying to understand the business process and getting the business to rationalize their own processes, before letting it flow across that boundary and ending up forcing us to create a hodgepodge in IT systems. And the partnership I create with the people who run the business ends up creating a better overall business system design.[7]

Another reminder of the importance of relationships.

A final illustration of this point may be the most telling. When AARP recently hired A. Barry Rand as CEO, one of the very first things he did—even before he began his first day on the job—was to call CIO Matt Mitchell into his office to say, "So, tell me how our business runs."[8] Rand recognized that a smart CIO probably knows more about the realities of the end-to-end business than does any other executive.

PEOPLE LEADERSHIP (THE VALUE AMPLIFIER)

We have talked throughout about the importance of soft, or people, skills. As you know, as a leader, you can accomplish very little on your own. The only way to achieve things of significance is through others, and that explains why (1) you need superior soft skills and (2) people leadership is the critical third leg of our three-legged value-creation stool, which includes business acumen and technological savvy.

But the people leadership leg is important for another reason. It is the biggest lever the modern CIO can pull to maximize the overall contribution he or she can make.

Sure, you can get better at understanding all aspects of the business, and you should. And certainly, learning more about the technology itself is helpful as well. But there really isn't any exponential benefit from doing either. In both instances, you are limited by how much better you become (i.e., how much more *you* learn about the technology; how much more *you* increase your understanding of the business). However, if you are able to persuade, lead, and otherwise influence others, then you get to leverage all *their* time, all *their* skills, and all *their* relationships to get done what needs to get done. You also gain their buy-in during the process. That's why the amount of value that a CIO delivers as head of the IT organization is a function of the combination of technological knowledge and business knowledge amplified by the executive's people-leadership skills.

Here's a quick example of why that is true. Think back to our discussion of business acumen. The CIO is usually the only person who sees across the entire business and therefore often truly understands the end-to-end business flow better than anyone else. This can be an incredibly powerful insight.

Many CIOs, however, do not have their people-leadership skills honed to a level to be able to translate this insight into business advantage. They cannot inspire, influence, or create a vision that they can bring to their colleagues and have them buy in. However, if these same CIOs can master people-leadership skills, great things can happen. They can help the organization

---

The best CIOs proactively influence their environment instead of reacting to it. They apply the full range of their people skills to collaboratively involve others, not only to shape the future, but to achieve a common vision and purpose.

FIGURE 8-1

The professional payoff

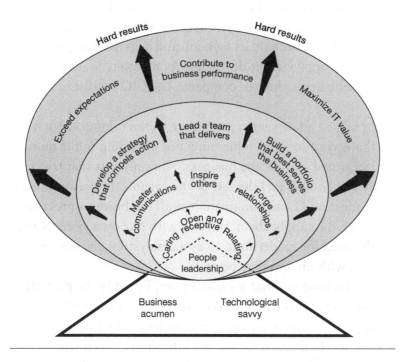

translate insights into action. It is the people-leadership skills that allow the connections to be made and the other pieces—technological and business insights—to come alive.

It is not that these CIOs who exercise the combinatorial advantage necessarily have one big idea. It's that they create the environment for others to generate, nurture, and ultimately realize the value from their ideas across the organization. The professional payoff, or the combinatorial advantage, amplified by people leadership, is shown in figure 8-1.

THE COMBINATORIAL ADVANTAGE IN ACTION

Here's an example that shows how the combinatorial advantage adds value. More specifically, it shows how people-leadership skills are the key to unlocking the underlying value from business acumen and technological savvy. The CIO of a global manufacturing firm (who asked to remain anonymous) had completed a multiyear IT turnaround that successfully proved his department's ability to both do its own job and help other departments within the organization do theirs. As a result, he had earned great credibility within the company. The CIO recalls:

> I realized a few years ago that we weren't doing enough in the way of long-term planning nor attending to the more integrated view of the business. Not only was that true for IT but [it held for] the rest of the organization as well. So I made it an IT mission to analyze all the business processes along the supply chain, starting with our own systems and the need for modernization as a catalyst for the conversation with my business peers.
>
> Because of what we had accomplished in the past, the company's most senior executives were open to this approach. I took my most high-potential IT leader, let's call her Katie, and moved her into this role as a stretch assignment. I supported her with consulting help for supply-chain knowledge, and I personally coached her along the way in critical people-leadership aspects such as developing executive relationships and how to communicate, collaborate, and influence at this level.
>
> It took about eighteen months, including mapping out and codifying the entire business process and how it could work moving forward. Once we figured it out, the questions were who was going to brief our chairman and our president, and what would be the best way to do it.
>
> I wanted Katie to lead this effort. She had been in charge of the project, and I wanted her to get the exposure and experience collaborating and developing relationships with the senior executive team.
>
> Her presentation really wouldn't be about technology, and ironically, that was probably the biggest issue we were

going to face at the meeting. People were going to assume we were going to come and present everything from an IT perspective.

But we would be actually presenting an organizational overview, because people just didn't have an appreciation of the problem beyond their own silos. To me this is the value that IT has. No other department is in the position to see the entire organization.

"Katie" picks up the story from there, and you will notice that she is about to deploy many of the social-participative leadership skills we discussed in chapter 2 and communication techniques we talked about in chapter 5.

The supply chain here is rather complex. You're talking from product planning, marketing, all the way down to manufacturing, logistics, and delivery to our customers. And a lot of people here have pieces of it; they don't see the whole thing of it. Except, of course, if you're IT.

But I have learned, through keeping the business executives up to date on the status of their projects, that their eyes always glaze over by about the third PowerPoint slide if the topic is not directly relevant to them. So the issue I had was communicating something very complex in a way that wouldn't bore people. Indeed, I needed to do it in a way that would engage them and cause them to be involved.

I have one whole wall in my office that is nothing but a whiteboard. I decided I'd sketch out there the entire business process and what we learned. I pulled out some key things I thought they would find interesting around product and supply chain complexity, customer retention, and so on. I drew pictures, and I used multiple colors to make key points. And when people made comments about what I was proposing we do, I would add their comments along the way. So I basically walked our key business executives, including our president and the chairman, through a story on my whiteboard.

At one point, our chairman stood up at the whiteboard and drew things while he was debating with me the best way to do something I was proposing. What was so fabulous about it was that it wasn't my idea against his; we were collaborating on the best solution.

The result of this collaborative process was that the core ideas proposed by the CIO and his protégé for end-to-end supply-chain process and systems optimization were adopted by the chairman. Indeed, the company hired a business vice president with responsibilities that spanned the whole supply chain to implement the needed business transformation and the upgrading of the enabling systems to go with it.

The payoff, as the CIO notes, was threefold:

1. The supply chain was optimized.

2. IT received recognition for its larger role in the business. "Given the success of the project," said the CIO, "the business side of the company has begun to see us in a new light. Key business executives now view IT as a collaborative and strategic partner, based on the value we helped identify and unlock."

3. Key people enhanced their professional development. "It was an absolutely wonderful growth experience for Katie as well" was the CIO's comment. "She's an entirely different person in terms of competency from even just five years ago, let alone twelve years ago, and that is important because I can't do everything I want to alone. I need good people."

The last point is particularly important and worth stressing. This story is not just about the CIO's intelligence to see an opportunity (i.e., "build the best mousetrap," an approach that we talked about in chapter 2). Rather it is really about his ability to lead, through employing the combinatorial advantage, in this case by building technology literacy with business peers and developing the next generation of IT leaders under the CIO. The net result is that the CIO increased his capacity and capability to create value on both an immediate and more sustainable basis. As we observed with him, and other high-performing CIOs, accomplishing extraordinary results via others is not only tremendously fulfilling, but also a key to work-life balance in the CIO role (more about this in the next chapter).

CREATING VALUE VIA RISK MANAGEMENT

Fortunately, the same combination of technological, business, and people leadership that allows you to capitalize on opportunities can also be used to leverage the opposite side of that coin—managing or minimizing risk. This capability is another example of how CIOs deliver value.

"I'm really focused on the precision with which we operate, embracing best practices and operations, and modeling ourselves to other high-performing industries," says Tim Zoph, CIO of Northwestern Memorial Hospital. "One of the responsibilities I recognize and fully accept is that once you drive technology deep into the organization, when it becomes part of the core of the enterprise, the business risk increases significantly. You have created a dependency, because you can no longer effectively operate without IT."[9]

In light of the combinatorial advantage we have been advocating, an excellent CIO has the opportunity to present risk to the business as exactly that—risk to the business: risk of a process breaking, of information leaking, of customers leaving, etc.

The point here can be easy to overlook. The value of technology is *optimized* when a CIO has the opportunity to do what's *right or best* for the enterprise. The best thing might be discarding technology in favor of merely implementing a process change, or agreeing to a single piece of technology across a global company, even though it means changing the business processes or delaying a project. And as Zoph points out, CIOs can also add value by minimizing the risk associated with both the technology and the process transformation and subsequent operations (finances, customer privacy, whatever) it enables.

That's a point worth underscoring. As companies become increasingly dependent on technology; as processes supported by technology cross company, industry, and national boundaries; as privacy issues abound; and as information becomes so pervasive, the systems the CIO's team manages can also do the greatest harm to the business. For this reason, CIOs must form deep, honest, and appropriate relationships with the business to ensure that risks are indeed being managed.

The combinatorial advantage works here as well. Because top CIOs perform so well at the intersection of people, technology, and business, they play a valuable role in both identifying risks and advising and collaborating with their peers so that the appropriate risk-mitigation precautions can be taken.

THE IMPORTANCE OF PASSION IN YOUR PROFESSIONAL LIFE

When we talk to the CIOs who love their job, and many do, we sense the real passion they have for making a positive difference. At some point during our interviews, the conversation would turn to the impact each wanted to make. When it did, the

---

The best CIOs use the same combination of technology, business know-how, and people skills to engage the business in the right conversations to ensure that organizational risk is managed effectively. Without that combination, risk mitigation is marginalized to firewalls and sign-ons.

CIOs' tone became more excited. They talked faster and often louder. Their passion was palpable. You could see that they truly wanted to create value.

They wanted to have an impact via IT. Whether that impact was contributing to developing a better drug for a customer; finding additional revenue for the company; changing their organization's business model within their industry; creating the most efficient end-to-end supply chain; or leaving a legacy of efficiency or improving their corner of the public sector, they all had—and continue to have—a passion for making a difference. They want to create significant value for their enterprise, as Randy Spratt puts it, "by helping successfully leverage technology, which is the tool we wield."

By combining exemplary "soft" people skills with your business acumen and technological savvy, you are able to do the job you signed up to do. For it is through this combinatorial advantage that you (and the other top CIOs) truly create value and deliver on IT's potential.

CALL TO ACTION

If you are still looking to grab hold of the people-skills lever as a way to amplify IT's value contribution, consider the following tips for development:

FREE YOURSELF UP.   There's no way you are going to be successful at developing your people skills if you remain stuck in the weeds and running around putting out fires. Get out of the technological side and into the people side of things. You can simultaneously accomplish each of these goals through delegation, which both frees up your time and develops your people.

SHARE WHAT YOU KNOW.   Similar to the above, investing in your people helps increase their capabilities and relieves time and pressure constraints. Along with delegation and ongoing mentoring and coaching of your people, the developing of IT literacy with your business partners will help to pass along the critical knowledge and skill that will enable them to contribute more. And you will have more time to hone your people skills to shape the future and lead strategically at the intersection of business and technology to maximize the value contribution from IT.

FOCUS YOUR INITIAL EFFORTS. If you haven't flipped the switch on your people skills just yet, don't go into full power mode right away. Pick a spot, preferably a project of moderate scope and difficulty, to apply your attention to developing your people skills in a focused manner. Apply your leadership skills as you normally do in other parallel areas. Over time, note the differences between these other projects and the project where you are focusing on leveraging your people skills. Bit by bit, start transferring those skills over to the other projects, making the necessary adjustments and applying the lessons learned from your other experiences.

DO MORE BY DOING LESS. We've covered this before, but it bears repeating. Get things accomplished not by focusing your efforts directly on the task at hand; get it done by working *through* other people. Let others do the majority of the heavy lifting while you stoke the fires of learning and motivation. This is no easy task in and of itself, but is a lot more effective in the long run.

SUMMING UP

In the IT industry, we have long talked about the unique opportunity we have as CIOs to see across the enterprise and identify value-creation opportunities. But it is one thing to see those opportunities and another to capitalize on them. To come up with ways that the business can not only improve its end-to-end processes or transform its business model, but can also actually implement technology-enabled innovation for business advantage—that is where the payoff is.

As we have seen, the best way to get things done is through a combination of technical know-how, business acumen, and people skills. More specifically, as CIO, you want to use your soft skills to leverage not only your business and technical expertise, but also the power of the extended team. If you are able to persuade, lead, and influence others, you can leverage all their time, all their skills, and all their abilities to deliver results and maximize the business value that has been enabled via IT. That is the biggest lever you can pull. It is the way to be truly effective as a CIO.

Given the pervasive nature of technology in the hyper-connnected enterprises of the twenty-first century, our C-suite peers, boards, and public-sector governing bodies are increasingly looking for a CIO who not only sees opportunities, but also is a strong, collaborative leader on the executive team, helping to realize the benefits and actually deliver on the promise of technology. As we have seen, you add the most value and are held in the highest esteem when you effectively unite your business, technological, and people skills into the combinatorial advantage. That's the true professional payoff: collaboratively delivering business results and the value of IT.

THE PERSONAL PAYOFF

GAINING GREATER FULFILLMENT INSIDE
AND OUTSIDE WORK

It is not just your department and enterprise that benefit from all the things that we have talked about so far. You do, too, both professionally—and personally. We've often observed that even good CIOs suffer from burnout. They have an intense drive to achieve results, but ironically, often because of the task-oriented leadership style that got them to the CIO role in the first place (see chapter 2), they now struggle to get it all done. What's more, it often affects all aspects of their life, public and private. But we have also observed that the great CIOs, the ones who are dedicated to people leadership first and who live the combinatorial advantage we just discussed in chapter 8, not only exceed expectations, but do so while achieving work-life balance. They get great fulfillment from their job.

Matt Mitchell, CIO of AARP, is proof of that: "Since my people can deal with the things that used to eat up my day— project reviews, meetings, and all the inevitable minor crises—I am free to work on strategy. I have the chance to think about the things we have to do to generate value, and I have the time

to figure out what I need to do to get the various affected stake-
holders committed to carrying it out. That's a far better use of
my time, and it is also much more satisfying."[1]

We've observed this pattern across the great CIOs. The
payoff from making people leadership your first priority is that
you (1) accomplish more, ironically by doing less yourself
(proving that the cliché of working smarter, not harder, is pos-
sible); (2) finally gain the opportunity to do the job you signed
up to do; (3) leave a legacy you are proud of; and (4) do all this
while gaining balance in your personal life. In short, your per-
sonal and professional life dramatically improves.

Let's see why this is true.

SOFT SKILLS YIELD hard results for you personally as well.
Until now, we have talked primarily about the payoff to the
organization if you hone your interpersonal skills. And indeed,
that payoff is huge. As we have seen, the use of your people-
leadership skills, in combination with your business and technological savvy, produces substantial benefits not only in the IT
department, but also organizationwide.

This is no small point. Indeed, as we have seen, this can be
the difference between spotting an opportunity to deploy technology on your organization's behalf for business advantage
and actually making it happen. But if you work at it—and as
you will see later in the chapter, you do have to make a commitment that may make you uncomfortable at first—you will benefit (dramatically) as well. You have the opportunity to become
more productive; you end up (finally) being able to do the job
you signed up to do; and, oh, by the way, you get your life back.

YOU ACCOMPLISH MORE BY DOING LESS

What is sometimes forgotten in our discussion of developing
your staff (see chapter 7) is that since you are drawing on the

A POTENTIALLY TROUBLING QUESTION

Good CIOs, while achieving much for their organization, often take on too much of the wrong work themselves and therefore run the very real risk of burning out.

Great CIOs are able to do the job they signed up to do. They can focus on a true people-leadership role and achieve extraordinary results via others, which allows them to find immense fulfillment in their work.

Which path are you traveling down?

improved skills of those around you, the IT department is able to get more of the right work done. That's a good thing since high-performing CIOs are high performers because they exceed expectations. They execute. They deliver results.

You can see the multiple benefits that naturally flow from this:

- You become more accomplished, so you feel better about the job.

- Your team is happier since you are giving people a chance to learn and grow.

- Your business partners are more satisfied because you are working with them collaboratively, assisting them in accomplishing their critical business goals via enabling IT solutions. You aren't an order taker; you are a vital part of their success.

These benefits feed upon themselves, making a virtuous circle, and the irony is that by being able to stay out of the details (things that are handled by your staff), you can accomplish far more. Just about all your time is truly productive. You are focusing on the right things. Instead of reacting to problems, you are creating an environment for success.

If this is not your reality today, just pause for a moment and imagine what would happen if you made it so. By implementing everything we have talked about, you could do the job you signed up for. You could have highly effective partnerships with your business peers; collaboratively create business-aligned IT strategy; and, most importantly, significantly contribute to delivering great value for your enterprise, instead of spending the majority of your days keeping the lights on and putting out technologically related problems.

That's possible, as we have seen, because of three reasons:

1. You have "the right people on the bus," and you have selected, developed, and empowered them (see chapter 7).

2. You have developed great relationships with your business counterparts both inside and outside the organization, so everyone is focused on the same goals and objectives. There is less internal strife (see chapter 4).

3. Because of points 1 and 2 and your commitment to the seven skills we have talked about throughout this book, you have earned the respect of your peers and are treated as a full partner in shaping the fate of the enterprise.

Point 3 is worth underscoring: by educating your business partners and working with them early on to develop ideas, you have more influence; instead of constantly reacting to situations, you have the opportunity to shape the environment in which you operate. That will allow you to find, as AARP's Mitchell did, true fulfillment in your work because you will be doing the work you have wanted to do from the beginning. Our research shows the best CIOs are also the ones who find their jobs extremely satisfying, enjoy the most recognition and advancement, and suffer the least from burnout.

YOU LEAVE A LASTING—AND
LAUDABLE—LEGACY

"I really enjoy building high-performing teams that produce a competitive advantage for the company," says Duffy Mees, CIO of Promontory Interfinancial Network. "And I love to watch the people who work for me grow and develop."[2] Mees efficiently summarizes a constant thought we heard throughout our interviews.

Innumerable times, we heard CIOs tell us how happy they were to contribute to the success of others. We could see how they gained huge amounts of personal satisfaction in watching their people succeed. It was clear they had a great sense of pride, passion, and deep emotional fulfillment when they could truly make a difference in someone else's career or life, or both. And ultimately, of course, the success of your people is one of the most enduring legacies you leave behind. As Tim Zoph, CIO of Northwestern Memorial Hospital, puts it, "the people I help develop will have a big impact long after me."[3]

And "people," in this case, can extend beyond IT. Because you have worked well with others throughout your company, employees organizationwide will have a better understanding of how the technology can be used for competitive advantage. This is another telling difference between great CIOs and those who are merely good. The great CIOs make it a core part of their role to develop technological literacy in their business partners. That is why these CIOs achieve way more in the short term and leave a far more enduring legacy.

What will your legacy be?

YOU GET YOUR PERSONAL LIFE BACK

As one of the CIOs we talked to put it when we asked about the personal payoff that honing your soft skills brings, "you get to tame the work-life-balance monster." Here's why.

The classic sign that your life is out of balance is when you can't "stay in the moment." You wish you were at home when you are at work, and when you are home, work concerns are uppermost in your mind. By gaining control over your work life and by doing all the things we have discussed, you can achieve something resembling a normal work life. The hours you work are more productive. You are able to concentrate on the things most appropriate to the CIO leadership role when you are at work and know things are under control when you leave the office—in this way, you actually enjoy your time off.

Now, this doesn't automatically get your life in balance. You need to commit to it. That begins by giving yourself permission to have a life outside the office. Ironically, if you don't, you end up suffering both at home and at work, since you burn yourself out. As Gerald Shields, CIO of Aflac, aptly explains:

> I think one of the biggest challenges of being a CIO is no matter how much you accomplished last year, there is that much more that must be accomplished this year. You think by working even harder, you can get ahead. Well, you are not going to get ahead.
>
> You have to pace yourself. This is a marathon. I ran the Chicago Marathon back in 2001, and I remember when I was preparing for it, people told me, "You need to drink at every water stop."
>
> I said, "Every water stop?"
>
> And they said, "Yeah, it's 26.2 miles. And you've got to prepare yourself to run the whole way."
>
> And if you look at who starts these marathons and then doesn't finish, it's those people who are not prepared to go the whole way, who are not drinking water every

mile. Those little things are what make you get all the way to the end. This isn't a sprint. It's a marathon.[4]

This is something that Dave Swartz, CIO of American University, learned firsthand:

Earlier in my career, I had an enormous amount of stress, which had begun to manifest in my family, too. I was taking my problems home. I decided to change. I gave myself permission to focus more on my needs and forced myself to understand there was more to life than work. I started delegating more, making sure I was eating right and exercising. As a result, I found that situations I would have found to be most stressful in the past became challenges that were fun. It went from how am I going to deal with this, on top of everything else I have to do, to let's see what we can truly accomplish. It became like mountain climbing. You get an adrenalin rush. You get excited about the challenge in front of you, and you accomplish it.[5]

You benefit from all this, of course, but so does your company and your staff. First, *you have more energy when you are at work, and consequently more capacity to lead.* Equally important, by successfully delegating necessary work to your staff and consistently getting out of the office at a decent hour, you are modeling the kind of behavior you want.

Many talented people decide early in their career that they have absolutely no desire to become a chief information officer. They look at all the time their boss, the CIO, is putting in, and

---

What would your personal and professional life be like right now, if you had leveraged the power of people leadership first, in all its aspects, four or five years ago?

---

they say, "Not for me." This is obviously a concern for organizations in general and our profession specifically.

"If the job of CIO is presented in such a way that people cannot keep their life in balance, they may not choose our career," says Zoph. "So, I worry that if, one, we don't give people the tools or techniques for work-life balance or, two, we don't demonstrate that there can be work-life balance, we won't cultivate the leadership we need for a next generation. Life balance is about individual choices you make every day. Time is our most precious commodity in life; we need to use it well. Honoring the commitments you make to yourself builds character and authenticity: the foundations of being a leader. You need to define what's important to you first, before you can be an effective leader to others."

If your staff sees that you have created a normal work-life balance, then they may rethink their position that the CIO role will consume every aspect of their life. That will open up a much wider pool of qualified candidates.

IT ISN'T MAGIC: GREAT FOCUS
(ON THE RIGHT THINGS) REQUIRED

None of this occurs by accident. It takes great self-awareness and discipline to make each of these points a reality, but as Shields points out, that actually plays to your strengths:

> I'm very goal oriented. I think most successful CIOs are. And counterintuitive as it may seem, you have to set some "soft-side" goals—whether it is developing your people, making sure that you are spending enough time with your family, or both. We, as aggressive CIOs, need to make sure that we do not become so results oriented, so task oriented, that we lose balance in our lives.
>
> The strengths that typically get you to be a CIO of any decent-sized organization are your ability to focus

and deliver and to get things done. At the end of the day, that's what keeps you employed.

But the danger is, you will develop those strengths to the point where you will overuse them. You'll spend all your energies concentrating on what you have to get done at work. That's why we need to set goals for obtaining balance.

And one of the ways to achieve balance is developing your people to the point where they can pick up much of the burden. Richard Gius says his mentor, Kathy White, drilled this into his head long before he ever started believing that he would become a CIO: "She really helped me start thinking about how my legacy should not only be what we accomplish for the organization, but must include how well I built up a leadership staff, a bench of leaders within the IT organization who some-day would be able to succeed me. She made it clear that if I left the organization and didn't have a clear successor, then I would have failed in a critical way."[6] The takeaway from these four points is clear: both you and your organization will thrive if you can master the things we have talked about throughout this book. As Zoph puts it, "It's all about choices that we make on a day-to-day basis. If I'm making the right choices, and I'm happy about those choices, and I feel like my life is in balance, it comes through in my leadership."

Soft skills really do yield hard results.

COMING FULL CIRCLE: SUMMING UP

Figure 9-1 summarizes everything we have talked about so far in this book. (You'll note this is the same illustration as figure I-5 in the introduction.) Let us take a moment here to underscore what we have learned about the specific leadership skills necessary to drive results.

Chapter 1 showed that by committing to put people leader-ship first, high performers build the foundation on which all

FIGURE 9-1

The CIO edge

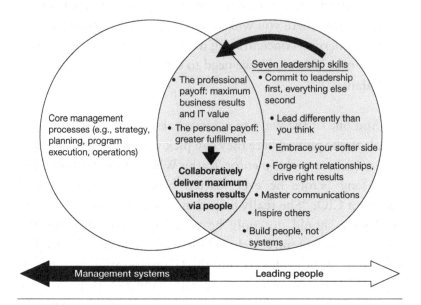

other success lies. Their intellectual and emotional commitment to leading through and with other people prepares these leaders to deal with the increasing complexities they face.

In chapter 2, we learned that once they make the commitment to lead through, by, and with people, the best CIOs open themselves to the realization that the leadership style that initially moved them up the ranks is not going to be the one that enables success in a senior management position; they now need to lead in a style that differs from the way they think. They still leverage their intellect, but now they collaboratively drive business results by using a much more social-participative leadership style.

By embracing their soft side—through being open, caring, and relatable—they create a connectedness that fully engages everyone around them. That was the lesson of chapter 3.

As we saw in chapter 4, they use that ability to help forge the right relationships—especially the horizontal ones—which gives them the ability to draw on and leverage the entire people network they create.

An effective network of people is made possible, in part, through artful communications, the subject of chapter 5. By using consistency of purpose, listening to and understanding each person's context and responding in kind, and embracing people's nonverbal ways of communicating, successful leaders are able to get their message across in ways that are felt, not just understood. This optimizes results because it compels people to take the right actions.

High-performing CIOs also get people to take the right actions through inspiration, as we saw in chapter 6. They inspire others by creating a vision that resonates with each person, and then they turn it into reality by building teams that have shared purpose and motivating people to perform their best.

And top performers are constantly developing people, the subject of chapter 7. Whether it is themselves, through open and honest feedback loops; their organization, through coaching and experiential learning; or their partners, through increasing IT literacy, they create an expanding and sustainable base of talent that provides the best possible return from the business's investment in IT.

By using the superior people skills you have developed to amplify the impact of both your business knowledge and your technical knowledge, you are able to achieve more professionally, as we saw in chapter 8. Not only can you meet expectations, but you can also make a true difference and deliver extraordinary value organizationwide. You are no longer seen solely as the person in charge of technology, but are also viewed as a highly effective business leader who knows how to collaboratively partner to wield technology for business advantage. As a result, you can justifiably take great pride in your team (both immediate and extended) and the results it helps to produce.

It is rare when taking a specific course of action results in benefits across the board. But soft skills really do produce hard results for both you and your organization.

We have ended the book with this chapter on personal pay-off for a reason. It's your personal goals that will determine what you do next.

CALL TO ACTION

There's just one thing left to say:

MAKE IT PERSONAL. A call to action is meaningless unless you are truly motivated to act. We have done our best to give you the knowledge, insight, and skill-building tips necessary to prepare you to move from good to great as a CIO. Now it's up to you.

If you decide to improve your soft skills, to increase hard, tangible results—and we hope you do—remember, it won't be easy. It will require a real commitment. Our suggestion? Think less about the challenge and what you might sacrifice in your efforts to grow and more about what you will gain. Think how this will benefit you, your people in the organization, and your family. If that means enough to you, then you're ready for the next step.

AN OVERVIEW OF THE RESEARCH

The conclusions presented in this book are the result of empirical research, qualitative data, in-depth interviews, observation, and experience. Each source was analyzed for patterns and subsequently validated against each of the other sources. We engaged in this cyclical and multidimensional analysis to guarantee the rigor and depth of our conclusions.

Our foundational research on executive leadership came from a combination of empirical data from KFI's proprietary StyleView assessment methodology and normative data from KFI's Lominger research. StyleView benchmarks executives' thinking and leading styles and their emotional demeanor against a pattern of best-in-class executives (best-in-class patterns exist for almost all functions within a company such as CEO, chief financial officer, CIO, controller, and vice president of sales). These best-in-class patterns had been determined by analyzing an initial set of 120,000 executives (at the time of publication, this database contained over 1.4 million records) for the behavioral qualities that lead to success. When the standard analysis of variance was computed on these patterns, the differences were all statistically significant. We focused on the pattern of best-in-class CIOs.

We then analyzed KFI's Lominger competency research as it related to the best-in-class CIO pattern. Lominger's library of competencies is empirically mapped to the StyleView framework, enabling the translation of a best-in-class profile to a rank-ordering of competencies that are critical for success. Our observations were further informed by Lominger's ongoing global norms and validity research, which determines the competencies most strongly correlated with success at different organizational levels and also rank-orders competencies by perceived skill and importance to success.

Gartner, Inc., research also played heavily throughout the research. Besides the empirical data from KFI/Lominger, we also analyzed the deep, CIO-specific research within Gartner and its Executive Programs Division (EXP). The executive research conducted by Gartner includes an extensive annual CIO survey (the 2010 CIO research report was based on the participation of 1,600 CIOs responsible for more than $120 billion in corporate and public-sector IT spending), plus extensive case-based discrete research projects focused on key themes identified via the annual survey and of most interest to CIOs. All of this is supplemented by ongoing observation (i.e., thousands of client inquiries and interviews annually) and the knowledge of Gartner's highly experienced analysts.

The research agenda covers the multiple roles of today's CIO: business leader, keeper of technology, business partner, change agent, and so forth. It also analyzes the role of the CIO from a future perspective: the impact of social, technological, and economic trends on businesses and IT and, therefore, the CIO. Examples of specific Gartner research and EXP projects drawn on in this book include the following reports prepared by the company: "Identifying CEO Expectations and Delivering Against Them"; "Hyperconnected Enterprise: Demand for Advanced Leadership Explodes"; "Leading Beyond Now: Techniques to Manage Transformation and Change"; and "CIO Political Landmines and How to Avoid Them."

Given a best-in-class pattern for CIOs from a thinking and leading perspective, the list of the Lominger competencies best associated with that pattern, and Gartner's wealth of CIO research, we sought to interpret the data in the context of acting CIOs through in-depth interviews. Our target CIOs came from the Korn/Ferry database, Gartner's broad CIO client base, and recommendations drawing on our combined extensive global industry networks. For the Korn/Ferry database, we identified CIOs whose assessment matched that of absolute best in class and those who didn't. The Gartner nominations were CIOs who had not necessarily taken the assessment, but had a reputation of excellent leadership. We reference-checked this group to ensure that the reputation was well deserved. All CIOs were interviewed at length, using the same open-ended questions, to gather their opinions on many aspects of leadership, stories of their own experiences and lessons learned, and feedback on the initial conclusions drawn from the data.

After the initial interviews, the transcripts were content-analyzed for patterns. Additionally, we applied our own experiences and knowledge to the analysis, having worked within the IT industry as IT executives, CIO coaches, or expert analysts of the CIO role. Having identified a core set of themes and initial conclusions, we followed a parallel process of secondary interviews and "road-testing" our conclusions. We presented our initial findings to CIOs in ten cities; these CIOs represented an additional 150-plus companies of various industries, sizes, and ages. Discussion and feedback were consistently supportive of our initial conclusions. We also continued the one-on-one interviewing with secondary interviews of many CIOs, and interviews with their superiors or partners, again testing our conclusions.

The results are what you hold in your hands: a deep foundation of empirical research augmented with extensive, qualitative data gathering and experiential knowledge. The combination has given us a powerful view of what the most effective CIOs do differently than the majority of CIOs.

NOTES

INTRODUCTION

1. The discussion of Procter & Gamble throughout this book comes from a series of authors' interviews with Filippo Passerini and Lucy Hodgson between January and May 2009.

2. We thank Gartner, Inc., vice president Mark McDonald for his unknowing contribution to the Venn diagrams you will find throughout the book. Mark's talk "Leading Beyond Now: Techniques to Manage Transformation and Change," presented at the CIO Program at Gartner Symposium/ITxpo, Orlando, October 22, 2009, though in a different area, helped sparked what you see here.

CHAPTER 1

1. The discussions of Tom Tabor of Highmark throughout this book come from a series of interviews and correspondence the authors conducted with Dr. Ken Melani, Tom Tabor, Chuck Klein, and Kathy Martin between May and August 2009.

2. The discussions of Northwestern Memorial Hospital throughout this book come from a series of interviews the authors conducted with CIO Tim Zoph, CEO Dean Harrison, between January and June 2009.

3. Randy Spratt, telephone interview with authors, February 2009.

4. The discussions of Toyota throughout this book come from a series of interviews the authors conducted with Barbra Cooper and Karen Nocket between January and May 2009.

5. Shinji Hasejima, phone interview with author, tape recording, January 2009.

6. Ramón Baez, phone interview with authors, tape recording, March 2009.

7. Nick Smither, phone interview with authors, tape recording, February 2009.

8. Michael Kollig, phone interview with authors, tape recording, April 2009.

CHAPTER 2

1. Stephen Fugale, telephone interview with authors, tape recording, April 2009.

2. Stein Tumert, telephone interview with authors, tape recording, November 2009.

3. K. R. Brousseau, M. J. Driver, G. Hourihan, and R. Larsson, "The Seasoned Executive's Decision-Making Style," *Harvard Business Review*, February 2006, 111–121.

4. Pascal Buffard, telephone interview with authors, tape recording, November 2009.

5. Beth Perlman, telephone interview with authors, June 2009.

CHAPTER 3

1. Carol Zierhoffer, telephone interview with authors, tape recording, April 2009.

2. Ramón Baez, telephone interview with authors, tape recording, March 2009.

3. Ross Philo, telephone interview with authors, June 2009.

4. Duffy Mees, telephone interview with authors, May 2009.

CHAPTER 4

1. Robert Runcie, telephone interview with authors, tape recording, January 2009.

2. Dean Harrison, telephone interview with authors, tape recording, April 2009.

3. Carol Zierhoffer, telephone interview with authors, tape recording, April 2009.

4. Dave Swartz, telephone interview with authors, tape recording, February 2009.

5. Steve Stone, telephone interview with authors, tape recording, July 2009.

6. Colleen Young and Dave Aron, "Identifying CEO Expectations and Delivering Against Them," Gartner Executive Programs Report, August 2009.

7. Dick Gochnauer, telephone interviews with authors, tape recording, supplemented with written correspondence to authors, February and March 2009.

8. Dave Bent, telephone interviews with authors, tape recording, supplemented with written correspondence to authors, February and March 2010.

9. Marv Adams, telephone interview with authors, tape recording, February 2009.

10. Tom Tabor, telephone interview with authors, tape recording, August 2009.

CHAPTER 5

1. Owen McCall, telephone interview with the authors, tape recording, March 2009.

2. Richard Gius, telephone interview with the authors, tape recording, March 2009.

3. Gerald Shields, telephone interview with the authors, tape recording, February 2009.

4. Sherry Aaholm, telephone interview with the authors, tape recording, February 2009.

5. Filippo Passerini, telephone interview with the authors, tape recording, May 2009.

6. Ramón Baez, telephone interview with the authors, tape recording, December 2008.

7. Ross Philo, telephone interview with the authors, tape recording, June 2009.

8. Dean Harrison, telephone interview with the authors, tape recording, May 2009.

9. Sandra Camelo dos Santos, telephone interview with the authors, tape recording, May 2009.

CHAPTER 6

1. Marv Adams, telephone interview with the authors, tape recording, February 2009.

2. Phil Pavitt, telephone interview with the authors, tape recording, February 2010.

3. Sherry Aaholm, telephone interview with the authors, tape recording, January 2010.

4. Richard Gius, telephone interview with the authors, tape recording, February 2009.

5. Ramón Baez, telephone interview with the authors, tape recording, January 2009.

6. Filippo Passerini, telephone interview with the authors, tape recording, March 2009.

7. Tim Zoph, telephone interview with the authors, tape recording, March 2009.

8. Karen Nocket, telephone interview with the authors, tape recording, May 2009.

9. John F. Kennedy, "Space," section 9 in "Special Message to the Congress on Urgent National Needs," speech to joint session of Congress, May 25, 1961, John F. Kennedy Presidential Library, Historical Resources Archives, http://www.jfklibrary.org/Historical+Resources/Archives/Reference+Desk/Speeches/JFK/Urgent+National+Needs+Page+4.htm.

10. Dean Harrison, telephone interview with the authors, tape recording, May 2009.

11. Randy Spratt, telephone interview with the authors, tape recording, February 2009.

12. Richard Chapman, telephone interview with the authors, tape recording, February 2009.

CHAPTER 7

1. Gerald Shields, telephone interview with the authors, tape recording, April 2009.

2. Barbra Cooper, telephone interview with the authors, tape recording, May 2009.

3. Tim Zoph, telephone interview with the authors, tape recording, January 2009.

4. Robert Runcie, telephone interview with the authors, tape recording, March 2009.

5. M. M. Lomdardo and R. E. Eichinger, *The Leadership Machine* (Minneapolis: Lominger International—A Korn/Ferry Company, 2004).

6. Karen Nocket, telephone interview with the authors, tape recording, May 2009.

7. Filippo Passerini, telephone interview with the authors, tape recording, January 2009.

8. Shinji Hasejima, telephone interview with the authors, tape recording, January 2009.

9. Ramón Baez, telephone interview with the authors, tape recording, December 2008.

CHAPTER 8

1. Thomas G. Day, telephone interview with the authors, tape recording, June 2009.

2. Ross Philo, telephone interview with the authors, tape recording, June 2009.

3. Dave Swartz, telephone interview with the authors, tape recording, March 2009.

4. Sherry Aaholm, telephone interview with the authors, tape recording, March 2009.

5. Carol Zierhoffer, telephone interview with the authors, tape recording, April 2009.

6. Gerald Shields, telephone interview with the authors, tape recording, March 2009.

7. Marv Adams, telephone interview with the authors, tape recording, February 2009.

8. Matt Mitchell, telephone interview with the authors, tape recording, January 2009.

9. Tim Zoph, telephone interview with the authors, tape recording, April 2009.

CHAPTER 9

1. Matt Mitchell, telephone interview with the authors, tape recording, January 2009.

2. Duffy Mees, telephone interview with the authors, tape recording, August 2009.

3. Tim Zoph, telephone interview with the authors, tape recording, June 2009.

4. Gerald Shields, telephone interview with the authors, tape recording, May 2009.

5. Dave Swartz, telephone interview with the authors, tape recording, March 2009.

6. Richard Gius, telephone interview with the authors, tape recording, March 2009.

ACKNOWLEDGMENTS

Unless you have gone through the process, it can sound clichéd to say that writing a book that draws on such a broad research base is truly a team effort involving dozens of people whose names don't appear on the cover. But as we have discovered the cliché is true. This book was a collaborative effort.

We want to especially thank all the CIOs, CEOs, and other executives who contributed their time, enthusiasm, experience, and insights. Although they are quoted throughout, we would like to publicly thank them here. Our sincere thanks go to: Sherry Aaholm, Marv Adams, Ramón Baez, Dave Bent, Pascal Buffard, Sandra Camelo dos Santos, Rich Chapman, Barbra Cooper, Thomas G. Day, Stephen Fugale, Richard Gius, Dick Gochnauer, Shinji Hasejima, Michael Kollig, Dean Harrison, Ken Melani, Owen McCall, Duffy Mees, Matt Mitchell, Karen Nocket, Phil Pavitt, Filippo Passerini, Beth Perlman, Ross Philo, Robert Runcie, Dave Swartz, Gerald Shields, Nick Smither, Randy Spratt, Steve Stone, Tom Tabor, Stein Tumert, Carol Zierhoffer, and Tim Zoph. We are deeply thankful to each for generously giving us their time and thoughts.

We would also like to thank the numerous additional high-performing CIOs who also supported our research via interviews and collaboration; however, the laws of physics and page counts prevented us from being able to include them in the final book. Lastly, we want to acknowledge those who remain anonymous. They know who they are, and we are grateful for their help. Our conversations with all these people—credited or not—were inspirational. It was truly a privilege to experience their passion for people leadership and willingness to give something back to the CIO/ IT profession they (and we) love, in order to help inspire the next generation of business technology leaders.

Graham's colleagues at Gartner have provided great support, encouragement, and a wealth of research regarding CIO trends and best practices. Immeasurable thanks goes to Richard Hunter, vice president and Gartner Fellow, who was simultaneously a great supporter of the project, source of cutting-edge insight, and coordinator across Gartner's vast array of research resources. Particular thanks go to the Gartner analyst community for both their collaboration and contribution via their published research. We would especially like to acknowledge: Dave Aron, Diane Berry, Heather Colella, Linda Cohen, Ellen Kitzis, Mark McDonald, Lily Mok, Diane Morello, Tina Nunno, and Colleen Young.

In addition, Graham would like to thank Dale Kutnick, for his executive sponsorship and belief in this project, along with other members of EXP management, Jose Ruggero, Mary Ann Maxwell, and Toni Edelstein, who enabled this to happen. In addition, he wants to acknowledge his colleagues in EXP service delivery—Steve Weber, Bill Jenks, Al Passori, Louis Boyle, Jean-Louis Previdi, Bill Caffrey, and many others—who added their rich insight as experienced CIOs and were a constant source of encouragement.

Karen would like to give special thanks to Mark Polansky, managing director of Korn/Ferry's Information Technology Officers practice, and Kevin McNerney, formerly the managing director of the Reston Korn/Ferry office, who initially understood the power of developing cutting-edge intellectual property, encouraging Karen to write the book and supporting her in difficult times.

What makes this book different is the deep, empirical research at its base. This research led us to the initial understanding of how the best of the best have a clearly distinct way of always putting people first, regardless of whether or not the problem was technological, organizational, financial, or otherwise.

For this, we are extremely grateful to Korn/Ferry International (KFI) for giving us the statistically sound data patterns of high-performing executives. We would like to acknowledge the generous contribution of Stuart Kaplan, Peter Dunn, Dana Landis, Hawlan Ng, and Kim Ruyle.

And we are grateful to Bill King of KFI for seeing the value in this endeavor and supporting our pursuit of it.

We would like to thank Jacqueline Murphy and Kathleen Carr at Harvard Business Review Press for their editorial expertise and support. Heather Pemberton Levy of Gartner's book program deserves to be similarly acknowledged both for her editorial insight and for her patience and proficiency as we navigated the book-creation process.

And speaking of the book's creation, we offer a special thanks to Paul B. Brown. We would have probably hurt each other long ago if it weren't for his consistent level head, mastery of the English language, and perfectly timed sense of humor. And we would like to offer a huge shout-out—do they still say that, Katie?—to Katie Smith, age twelve, for her technical support.

Finally, it may seem strange to acknowledge your own coauthors, but truly little would have been done without the others: we all came to the project with a passion for the topic of people leadership; that's why we got together in the first place. Graham's unending attention to detail always got us to push for the "aha" moments among the data; Karen's insights helped us reduce the key messages to what would be clear and relevant to our core audience; and George repeatedly found the themes that pulled all the pieces together and provided deep and rigorous insights into the KFI-related data.

What doesn't seem strange is thanking you for reading.

Thank you.

INDEX

ABOUT THE AUTHORS

Graham Waller is a Vice President and Executive Partner with Gartner Executive Programs. He supports and is a trusted adviser to CIOs across a variety of industries, assisting them in business-IT alignment and maximizing IT value. He came to Gartner as part of the firm's acquisition of META Group, where he led CIO-level research on transformational change.

For more than twenty years, Graham has been driving business results and achieving measurable value from IT-enabled transformation. He has held both IT and business leadership positions within end-user and IT service provider *Fortune* 100 companies, including direct responsibility in the major disciplines of strategy, governance, IT portfolio management, e-commerce, and CRM.

He holds a bachelor's degree in electrical engineering from the University of Liverpool and a certification in e-business strategy from the University of Chicago.

George Hallenbeck is Director, Intellectual Property Development, for Korn/Ferry Leadership and Talent Consulting. With over a dozen years of experience in the field of talent management, he is responsible for the development of intellectual property (IP) that supports Leadership and Talent Consulting's service offerings and commercial products. He has coauthored the Lominger publications *Interviewing Right: How Science Can Sharpen Your Interviewing Accuracy* and the forthcoming *FYI for Insight*. He has expertise in developing IP in the areas of succession planning, coaching, and 360-degree feedback. He is a frequent speaker on emerging trends and critical issues in talent and has authored or coauthored numerous white papers and scientific articles.

He has an MS and PhD in industrial and organizational psychology from Colorado State University as well as a BS from Colby College in psychology.

Karen M. Rubenstrunk has led research on critical issues such as executive relationship management, leadership development, value management, organization development, and governance. Many of her client CIOs have received awards for Top CIO, Best Place to Work in Information Technology, Most Innovative CIO, and The Resourceful 100. Prior to joining Korn/Ferry's CIO practice, she successfully built META Group's executive offerings, including its highly successful CIO practice, before the company was acquired by Gartner.

She is a sought-after speaker on CIO leadership, able to hit at the heart of the issue with, as one CIO put it, "knowledge and compassion."

She holds a master's degree in business administration from Old Dominion University and a bachelor of science degree in business information systems from Arizona State University.